How to Hire Superstars for Your Day Nursery

Imogen Edmunds Chartered FCIPD

About The Author

Born in Chelmsford, Essex in 1973, Imogen Edmunds has spent over 20 years in Human Resource management, the last 12 years as Managing Director of Redwing Solutions Ltd, a HR and Training Consultancy based in Redditch, Worcestershire.

Redwing Solution's specialises in HR for Early Years and works with Day Nurseries, Pre-schools and Out of Hours Clubs across the Country.

Imogen has vast experience of supporting Nursery Owners, Directors and Managers with a range of HR and Employment Law issues.

Imogen is married to Stewart and has one son, James. Outside of work you will find Imogen involved in her local branch of National Association of Ladies' Circles and relaxing with a good coffee.

www.redwing-solutions.co.uk

Acknowledgements

I would like to thank my immediate family, Stewart, James and Mum and Dad for their support whilst I have spent my spare time being dedicated to the creation of this book.

Thank you for your support and patience and your belief that I would get it finished!

Chapters

Foreword

Finding the right staff to employ in your nursery has always been a difficult task and has become more so in recent times with the changes to GCSE qualifications and Paediatric First Aid requirements – it becomes more difficult to know just who you can count as qualified in your nursery, let alone being able to recruit them. So getting things right from the start of your recruitment campaign is obviously much more essential nowadays than ever before. And making sure you have considered all the factors that you need to, in order to undertake the successful recruitment of your Superstar, becomes just as important.

I have known Imogen professionally for many years now and her enthusiasm, professionalism and knowledge of HR and employment law shine through consistently, she advises on everything from recruitment of staff through to managing them and all the paperwork in between. So when she told me she was writing this book I thought what better person was there than her to do this!

And I was right...

Having read the book, I realised her insights into what makes nursery staff tick is brilliant and must be born from the many hours she has spent understanding their wants, needs and reasons for taking or leaving a job. She walks you through, taking you by the hand, each and every step of what to do in order to recruit the right staff members for your team to do the job you want them to do. She leaves no stone unturned.

In fact I was relieved to see, for the most part, I have been getting things right. However, even for those of us who have been recruiting for many years and think we have all the bases covered, there are some insightful new ideas and concepts and, for me, several reminders of things I need to revisit and review. This informative book also highlights the many myths within HR alongside what is best practice. Make sure you have your notepad to hand when reading it, for you will surely need it.

Tricia Wellings
Chief Executive
Bright Kids Day Nurseries

July 2016

Introduction

With an inflation busting National Living Wage just introduced in the UK, said to hike a providers costs by around a third, it's never been a tougher time to be recruiting for your Day Nursery.

In a profession which tends to be highly skilled and low paid, unqualified workers over 25 years of age, will be paid a minimum of £7.20 per hour likely to increase over the next four years to around £9 per hour by 2020 if the Government achieves its plans.

Deborah Lawson, general secretary of education and childcare union, Voice, said "Childcare's greatest challenge is recruiting and retaining staff. Raising the status of status of early years' professionals, as the Government claims it is doing, must go hand-in-hand with appropriate investment and coherent pay and career structures to reflect and reward."

Employers in this sector continually tell me how difficult it is to hire good quality staff, and how disappointing it is when good staff leave the sector because of the pay and conditions.

This book has been written out of my passion for your sector. As an independent HR Consultant I am fortunate enough to work with many Day Nurseries and I see every day the difference your teams make to the young people and parents you serve.

In addition to the National Living Wage we will soon see the introduction of 30 hours funded childcare for three and four year olds, in trial areas of the Country. I believe should this be rolled out, that this will certainly spell closure for some settings due to the current inadequate funding.

Closure may mean that the displaced staff will be able to be 'picked up' by other settings, but it may also mean that people leave the sector; perhaps for good.

In a sector where your front door can be literally locked shut by a third party, with huge amounts of bureaucracy and red tape, recruitment is a constant for many settings and unlikely to change any time soon.

If you are reading this book, I believe you are looking for ideas to help you to hire the best talent for your Day Nursery. In this book I cover the entire journey from designing the role through to inducting the new hire into your setting.

I hope you find it useful.

For secret bonus material go to
http://howtohiresuperstarsforyourdaynursery.co.uk

Chapter 1

What is a Superstar?

It's a known fact; not all employees are created equal.

Some employees probably give you headaches from time to time.

Pareto, an Italian economist gave us Pareto's Law. In Pareto's Law 80% of our issues would come from 20% of our employees. This may be true of you and your setting.

When we think about hiring superstars for your Day Nursery, we need to think about what are the characteristics that make someone a Superstar?

If I think about Superstars I have a mental picture of someone who is motivated, capable and works well with others. They inspire others; regularly have a big smile on their faces and the children and parents love them.

Superstars love Mondays. They are engaged with the organisation and share your values and beliefs.

They are the member of staff who you can rely upon; they are consistently effective (and not just when you are watching!). They are there when you need them; they turn up on a weekend to give their own time to improve the setting.

They identify what needs to be done and have it handled before you can mention it. When they do the order for the shopping, they've already sourced the most cost effective solution and spend your money as if it was their own.

They just get it! Whatever *it* is!

They give you confidence and are the core of your team. They may still be developing as practitioners but you know they will be excellent one day. If anything you fear that you won't be able to satisfy their aspirations forever, and one day they will leave you for pastures new.

We want you to hire Superstars. No one else is good enough for your Day Nursery, your children, your parents, and your existing staff.

In the current Statutory Framework for the Early Years Foundation Stage there is mention of 'suitable people'. In paragraph, 3.9 it is stated;

"Providers must ensure that people looking after children are suitable to fulfil the requirements of their roles. Providers must have effective systems in place to ensure that practitioners, and any other person who is likely to have regular contact with children (including those living or working on the premises), are suitable."

Suitable people may be fit to work with children, but that doesn't mean that they will be your Superstars.

Superstars! Join teams and they thrive. They enthuse others with their love of children and readily pass on their skills, knowledge and competencies to their colleagues, enhancing your setting all the time.

Having Superstars is what will make the difference between a good setting and an outstanding one.

Let's find you some Superstars!

Chapter 2

Do I need to Hire?

"Hire Slow & Fire Fast"

Howard Schultz

This may seem a bit of a daft question when you are looking to hire new staff for your Day Nursery. Bear with me on this as it's a really important question in my opinion and one we should answer slowly and not in haste.

You see it's really important, before you embark on any recruitment campaign, to ask yourself if you really do need to hire.

There may be other, sometimes better options than hiring new staff.

It's not cool, to hire someone into a post you *may* need, or for a job you *might* design once they've arrived, it's seriously uncool, to have lots of staff with nothing to do.

Your options instead of recruiting an external candidate are:

- Promote from within.
- Get an agency temp in, (yes I know they are expensive, but so is recruitment).
- Extend a part timer's hours.

- Offer overtime to someone who wants additional hours but not permanently.
- Use a zero hours/bank employee to cover the hours you need covered temporarily.
- Perhaps don't hire for this position; have a move around and hire for another post.

There are a few things you should avoid at this point. It's not considered acceptable to have a volunteer doing a post that you would otherwise hire for and apprentices whilst an important part of many nurseries staffing policy, volunteers aren't instead of practitioners and are usually in addition to practitioners.

Internal promotion

It is more cost effective to retain staff than to go through the costly process of recruiting new staff. As we will talk about in the next Chapter, it is also damaging to have a low stability index for your setting, where many staff are short serving; and therefore relatively new to your Day Nursery.

It's an urban myth that you have to advertise a vacancy externally if you wish to recruit; you can just advertise internally and avoid advertising costs.

If you do determine to open the vacancy up to internal candidates then you must remember to have an open and robust recruitment and selection process. Plenty of Nursery Managers have told me over the years, that they were promoted without an interview as a competent Deputy and that once promoted their colleagues felt negativity towards them, because they hadn't had a chance to put 'through their hats in the ring'. You don't want to do that to your Superstars.

External recruitment

Recruitment is costly and when thinking about attracting Superstars, we want you to be really sure that you are in a position to offer employment to someone who fits this description.

A Superstar will be selecting *you* as much, if not more, than you are selecting *them*.

It is hard to withdrawn a job offer because you have changed your mind. It will always cost you and it may end up with you in court for breach of contract.

Manpower Planning

Look at your manpower planning. Yes, I know it's a throwback phrase from the 1980's but it's as relevant today as it was then, where I say 'man' I of course mean 'woman' as well.

An effective manpower plan tells you what you need, where you need it, how long you need it for and when you will need the member of staff to work in order to meet your manpower needs.

Effective resourcing is about having the right people, with the right skills, in the right place at the right time.

We recommend the use of a skill matrix in your Day Nursery to help you with your manpower planning.

Skills Matrices

A Skills Matrix may be created by Room/Department or by Location if you are a multi-location provider. Often staff numbers mean that it is reasonable to have the entire team on one skills matrix and this is most desirable for effective manpower planning.

Each column on a skill matrix represents a skill. Here there are four columns on show; you can have as many as you like. Common skills we see recorded on a skills matrix include:

- Paediatric First Aid
- Able to read using story sacks
- EpiPen

The employer then assesses each employee on their skill. Here you can see Amy Cotton is a level 4 'skilled' in all the four skills areas that are shown on this extract of the Skill Matrix.

8	Amy Cotton	Nursery Nurse	4	4	4	4
9	Sam Stone	Nursery Assistant				
10	Charlie Kee	Nursery Assistant				
11	Sammie Sullivan	Apprentice	1	4	3	3
Number of Competent Individuals Required on Shift			3	3	3	3
	Key:					
	1	Novice				
	2	Can work under supervision				
	3	Can work unsupervised				
	4	Skilled				
	5	Able to train others				

Figure 1

It can be very useful if, at the bottom of the skills matrix you can insert a line which states the required number of personnel to be on duty with that skill. This effectively means you can use the skills matrix for your manpower planning and can authorise holiday and leave requests on the basis of suitable cover being available to you.

A Skills Matrix will have other uses, besides manpower planning, they will include:

- A visual aid to who has what skills and competencies
- A training and development tool, motivating staff to enhance their skill set and upskill by seeing the skills and competencies of others.
- A visual reminder to deliver on the job training, for Room Leaders.
- A Training Plan for staff to see what's in the pipeline for their own development.
- Succession planning enabling the staff to see what skills and competencies are possessed by more senior personnel.

I like a Skills Matrix to include colours and numbers and to be visually attractive. I will display on A3 paper, landscape and put it in a location where all the staff can review it, as required. There's little point having a Skills Matrix and hiding it away in a drawer!

I will use the left hand side to list the staff names, and the right hand-side to display skills and competencies. I will include regular skills such as Paediatric First Aid and less regular skills such as Introducing Phonics and Story Sacks.

I will use the numbers to indicate how competent the individual is deemed to be in that skill or competency. For some the maximum skill level will be a three. For example; as only external courses are used, no staff member will be able to train others in Paediatric First Aid.

1. Novice (i.e. Training identified)
2. Can work under supervision (i.e. Training Started)
3. Can work unsupervised (Trained)
4. Skilled (Competent, Training Completed)
5. Able to train others (Fully trained and confident to pass the skill on)

Agency or Bank Staff

If your need is temporary or ad-hoc, then you may consider use of agency staff, or casual/bank hours contracts as a more effective solution than hiring a Superstar on to your payroll.

Don't forget casual staff may or may not be employees depending on how you contract with them. Those that you wish to retain on bank are often classed as zero hours contracts and need to have special written statements of terms and conditions prepared for them.

Overtime or a 'Reshuffle'

Overtime or an undertaking a restructure of existing staff which may address your manpower needs without needing to add more staff to the payroll.

When hiring staff it is useful to not assign them to a particular room. For example say you wanted to hire a qualified Early Years Practitioner into your Pre School Room. If you specify on their letter of offer and contract of employment that they work in the Pre School Room, they can, quite rightly expect to remain in the Pre School Room. In the future if you wish to move them and utilise their talents elsewhere you will require their agreement to vary their terms and conditions of employment.

Much better to just employ them as a EYP and be able to move them from room to room to meet the organisation's needs.

Chapter 3

Developing a Talent Management Strategy

As you will have no doubt heard, the war on talent is on. We know how difficult it is to hire staff for your Day Nursery, yet some people don't seem to have any problem. So why do some people not have a problem and what is their secret?

It's very likely those who have least drama when it comes to hiring new staff have developed a talent management strategy. They may not know it as that. Indeed it may not have a name at all. It will be just a series of steps and processes that they use consistently to effectively reduce the need to 'panic hire'.

Lots of organisations including Day Nurseries have a mission statement, and lots of them talk about their employee's being their greatest asset. They are right. These are service businesses, and its people that provide service. However when we delve a little deeper that may be actually doing very little to hold on to that asset and to retain it long into the future.

Having a talent management strategy is about looking at how the organisation attracts and retains its human talent and rather than moving from one ad-hoc activity to another. It's about having a set plan of what you will do to achieve your organisation's objectives.

Take a long term view

Talent management can't be rushed and is a long term growth strategy about reducing turnover and retained the best people you can. Organisations will often do this with a multi-element approach which will include:

- Coaching and mentoring
- Continuous Professional Development
- Development Opportunities such as Secondments
- An effective Communication Policy

It is useful to see the value in investing in your talent pipeline.

Promoting your Day Nursery as an **'Employer of Choice'** and being active in the market will always encourage individuals to consider joining you as their next employer.

The term Employer of Choice means that applicants are eager to work for you, that people envy your employees, that you receive unsolicited CV's in the post.

This is one reason why we need to be careful when handling candidates and their experience with the Day Nursery. If you reject a candidate, they will tell others about their experience with you as a potential employer. If their experience was positive, despite them not being selected this will be repeated to the people they talk to. These people are often like them, and it is likely that people who work in Day Nurseries speak to other people who work in the Early Years' sector. These could be your 'candidates of tomorrow', if you have created a favourable impression, so the better.

An Employer of Choice doesn't have to be a large employer. They are often local employers whose reputation for how they treat and retain their staff is recognised and known by local people.

Being an Employer of Choice saves money on its recruitment costs because candidates approach you. Did you know that 100% of employee's at Tesco were customers of Tesco before becoming employees of the well-known retailer? Tesco can save money on its recruitment advertising costs by recruiting for many posts in their stores, in their stores. You may not have many potential employees coming through your doors today as parents, or relatives of your children on roll, but who is to say that these people won't be candidates of tomorrow, or at least know people who will be. Like Tesco you could maximise on this relationship.

To enhance their reputation amongst candidates that don't have prior experience of the organisation, many employers have made a commitment to the Investors in People award and more recently the Sunday Times Best Employer's awards. These have categories for smaller businesses and not for profits.

Promote the Nursery as a local employer

Lots of people are looking for local work for local people. Not everyone drives or wants the cost of running a car.

Ask yourself whether you are exploiting opportunities as a local employer to put your name out there.

Local strategies can include:

- Supporting local Facebook groups where you live.
- Supporting the Young Enterprise Scheme in your area.
- Attending Local Careers & Jobs Fairs.
- Developing ties with the local FE College.
- Providing interviewers to schools providing interview experience to pupils.
- Attending local events where local people get together.
- Public relations events such as supporting national and local charitable events (Children in Need, Jeans for Genes Day etc.) which will give you invaluable opportunities for PR in the local papers and online.

One of the popular investments Day Nurseries make is to get a pop up banner made advertising the Nursery as a great place to work. These do not have to be expensive. For less than £90 you can get a pop up banner printed that can be used many times over at local Careers Fairs and Open Days.

Measure what's working and do more of it

There are many areas of the employment relationship that are indicative of what's happening with employee recruitment and retention. For example if your recruitment is not effective I would expect to see the following happening in your Day Nursery:

- Increased Absenteeism.
- Lower interest in Flexible Working.
- Long term sickness absences increasing (particularly Stress at Work).
- High Labour Turnover.
- Poor Stability.

Attract talent organically

Common to any organisation's talent management strategy will be a desire to attract talent organically. By this I mean attracting individuals to join you without spending money specifically on recruitment advertising.

This will often involve encouraging Superstar candidates to apply speculatively to the setting without paying for the application.

Larger chains of Nurseries have no difficulty in attracting numbers of candidates who speculatively enquire as to whether they have any suitable vacancies and perhaps ask for a CV to be retained 'on file'.

There's nothing to prevent smaller organisations inviting candidate to apply at all points in the year and offering to retain prospective candidate's information on file.

This could be via a Careers@ email address or a 'Work With Us' page on your website. Even where you have no vacancies, you can describe the individuals you seek and invite candidate to submit their CV if they are interested in working with you.

Could your current employees act as a conduit for potential applicants? We often get to know other people that we meet in our profession when networking, and remain friends outside of work. They may be connected on social media such as Facebook and Linkedin.

The introduction of an Employee Referral Scheme that I explain in Chapter 8 to attract applications from suitable candidates can be very effective and is well worth considering.

One word of warning, there is a risk when storing information about an individual and you need to ensure that the information is kept secure. Adopt a Data Protection Policy and ensure that you do not keep data that you do not have permission to keep and that you do not retain data any longer than is necessary. If these difficulties can be overcome the benefit to the prospective candidate and employer are clear. Who would not want a supply of qualified leads in a drawer?

Look to keep what you hire

It is worthwhile mentioning here that in a talent management strategy we also should look at whether the organisation is retaining its talent. There is little point hiring talent for it to quickly become disillusioned and leave you.

Stability is the measurement of how stable an organisation is. Instability is bad, stability is good. The stability index is a measure of how stable you are.

We calculate the stability index by the following calculation:

Number of Employees with less than 1 years' service

--- x 100

Number of Employees with more than 1 years' service

Here's a worked example for you. Smiley Childcare had ten staff with under a years' service and twelve staff with over a year's service on 31st December 2015. Their stability index was therefore; 10/12 x 100 = 83%. They are instable. By contrast Hope Nursery has three staff with under one years' service and seventeen staff with over a years' service on the 31st December 2015, they have a stability index of 18%. They are highly stable with sufficient 'churn' of staff to introduce new ideas to the team.

In Day Nurseries I often see one of two things; either very low labour turnover and high stability; where organisations very infrequently have a leaver and the vast majority of staff have over a years' service. Or I see very high labour turnover and low stability. In the first situation this is great for customer service and can be excellent for team morale. However, fresh ideas and new perspectives are missed and this can over time, impact the organisation's ability to reach its potential and achieve its objectives.

Unfortunately in organisations with high labour turnover and low stability customer experience is often poor and uncertainty impacts existing team morale. Quality of provision is affected and the organisation may fail to reach its potential.

The 'sweet spot' is some labour turnover and a good level of stability. You want the majority of your staff to have over a years' service but not all. You want fresh ideas and fresh personnel to bring new personalities, which when well recruited will positively impact the team dynamic.

To calculate labour turnover you need the following equation:

Total Number of Leavers in the Period*

$$\frac{\text{Total Number of Leavers in the Period*}}{\text{Average Number of People Employed in Total in the Period}} \times 100$$

Average Number of People Employed in Total in the Period

*a period can be anything you like, six months, twelve months or a calendar year is common.

Here's a worked example for you. Smiley Childcare employed an average of 23 staff in 2015. In January 2015 they had 20 and in December 2015 they had 24, 20 and 24 added together = 44, 44 divided by 2 is 22.

In 2015 they had 5 leavers. This figure included those who resigned, were dismissed and the cook who retired. This gives them a labour turnover percentage of 5/22 x 100 which is 23%. Now that may not seem that high, but it is a 1/5th of the workforce leaving in the year. That would create additional training costs, lower staff morale, disadvantage communications and negatively impact the customer. When there is a ready supply of labour, employers can cope with relatively high labour turnover percentages, when good quality hires are difficult to make, or where the organisation is trying to grow and expand, such labour turnover rates can make things very difficult indeed.

Conduct Exit Interviews

It's important to know why people leave your employment and not to assume that you know.

There are three options when it comes to exit interviews:

- Exit Interview with a Line Manager.
- A Leaver's Questionnaire (physical copy).
- A 'Survey Monkey' style on line questionnaire (these could be anonymous).

The Exit Interview

Exit Interviews are best conducted by a neutral individual or someone from a HR background. Line Managers can be a problem and the reason someone is leaving. The Line Manager's Line Manager may often be the Owner. Many individuals will say its uncomfortable speaking to the Owner as they paid the employee's wages and will sign the reference requests that follow.

Exit Interviews should be conducted as soon as possible after the employee gives notice of resignation. If desirable, it may be possible to turn their decision around as well as vital to establish the true reasons for leaving. I have known employees to make whistleblowing complaints in the exit interview and to allege bullying behaviours or allegations of abuse which have led to them deciding to resign their employment. Either way once information has been collected from the exit interview the employer can see if it can make changes to reduce the chance of someone else leaving.

Ensure you maintain confidentiality. Mark the notes of the interview as confidential. Ask the employee to sign the notes and offer them a copy of what they have discussed.

Leavers Questionnaire (Physical)

Leavers questionnaires are the 'lightest touch' approach to find out why an employee is leaving your employment. It's easier than arranging an exit interview but the data should still be treated as confidential.

During my career, I have often used a Leaver's Form and asked exiting employees to indicate the reasons for their resignation and to rank in order of importance. One form sticks out in memory as it had a reason of leaving as death of employee. Tough exit interview that one!

Here are some reasons for leaving you could include in your Leaver's Form and Questionnaire.

- Salary or Hourly rate.
- Responsibilities (wanted more or wanted less).
- Too much or too little work/ lack of job satisfaction.
- Hours of Work.
- Travel/Commute.

- Lack of resources.
- Non pay benefits such as holidays, discounted childcare etc.
- Better prospects for pay and reward.
- Leaving single site for multi-site operation.
- Career Progression Opportunities.
- New/Alternative Career.
- Return to Full Time Education.
- Lack of Training and Development.
- Poor Health, deteriorating medical conditions.
- Unattractive Uniform.
- Opportunity to work with different age of children.
- Promotion.
- Starting new qualification.
- Cost of Childcare/Availability of childcare sought.
- Refusal of Flexible Working Request.
- Restrictions (such as a no baby-sitting policy, not being able to have a second job in competition with Nursery).
- To Go Travelling/Career Break.
- Partner relocation.
- Partner Job means no longer needs to work.
- Caring responsibilities (parents, relatives, children).
- Poor relations with management.
- Difficulties with colleagues/personality clashes.
- Unresolved grievance.
- Health and Safety issues.
- Bullying and Harassment.
- Favouritism by a Line Manager.

- Poor Direction from Line Manager.
- Other reasons, please state.....................................

On line survey style leavers questionnaire

This is a straightforward thing to set up on sites such as www.surveymonkey.com and for a basic free survey you can ask 10 questions that are answered anonymously and can give you an invaluable insight into the reasons behind a leaver's decision to resign. From the data gathered you can produce pie and bar charts or an annual report on leaver's statistics.

Differing reasons for resignations

People will leave an organisation for a variety of reasons. It is uncommon for it to be just *one* reason and is often a combination of factors. You can ask leavers to give you their top three reasons for leaving or to choose as many reasons as they like and place in a rank order. The benefit of this approach is that it is quick and easy for the leaver to complete and therefore they are more likely to give you the time to complete the information. In addition you gain quantitative data that you can compare, year on year to see the most popular reasons for leaving the organisation. This then gives you areas you can focus on if you wish to reduce the voluntary leavers from the organisation.

Some of the reasons people give are personal and nothing the employer could affect. These can include:

- Health.

- Child changing school/going to school.
- Promotion of a partner (not needing to work).
- Relocation of a partner.
- Caring responsibilities, looking after elderly relatives, sick family members, children below school age.
- Change of career, sometimes people discover their 'Why?' and it's not working for you. Recently we heard of a teacher that is giving up the profession to be a wedding planner.
- Return to full time education – retraining for an alternative career or to become a teacher is common place in the Early Years sector.

Sometimes the reasons are something the employer could affect:

- Access to flexible working and work life balance.
- Pay and rewards not comparable with expectations of the post.
- Opportunities for progression in their career.
- Non pay benefits such as existence of a Pension Scheme, Discounted Childcare etc.

Audit what you are offering

Sometimes we don't realise what we do offer and therefore don't shout enough about it to potential recruits.

A good idea is to audit what you do have on offer and see whether your competitors have spotted something you have not.

Common audits throw up the following anomalies:

- No training plan, so individuals can't see what's in the pipeline for them.
- No succession plan, no evidence that the organisation is keen to grow its own talent.
- No appraisal scheme, no opportunity to discuss career progression with the employees outside of supervision.
- No Flexible Working Request Policy- so organisation doesn't really know what it can and can't do when someone makes a request, lots of potential for inconsistent practice.
- No history of career breaks or sabbaticals to encourage those who want to leave to return to work after their break.
- Lack of awareness of "atypical contracts" and their utilisation for example many employers aren't familiar with compressed hours, 9 day fortnights, annualised hours or assume that zero hours contracts are now banned and a thing of the past.

Non pay benefits

Non pay benefits are also known as perks or fringe benefits. They aren't the attendance bonus, or a bonus given when a setting achieves "outstanding", they are the benefits available to staff to enjoy as part of their employment at your setting. They include; Employee Assistance Programme, Company Sick Pay, generous holiday entitlements, paid meals, enhanced maternity pay, adoption pay and paternity pay and private health/medical insurance.

Many non-pay benefits are expensive for the employer to administrate, especially where small numbers of staff are employed. For this reason they are not common in the Early Years sector. In addition many salary sacrifice schemes that may be found in other sectors aren't adoptable in the Early Years sector due to low wages. You can't offer a salary sacrifice that would take an employee below the national minimum wage.

Some non-pay benefits are available. We have found that these are popular:

- Additional Day off for their Birthday.
- A Snow Day – A pre-planned, pre-booked November/December day off work for shopping.

The benefit of these two non-pay benefits is that the employer can cost, pre-plan and prepare for these absences and it is something that they employee can choose to share with their family or keep to themselves!

Where an organisation identifies its strategy towards the above it can then look to communicate that strategy to potential and actual employees. That's not the end of the story. The strategy needs to be reviewed and where necessary revised at appropriate frequency. Any strategy left un-reviewed is likely to become 'out of date' or 'uncompetitive' over time. Then the positives of the approach are lost and rather than it supporting staff retention it becomes a reason for staff turnover.

I would encourage organisations to involve their staff in their decision making process. The best people to identify which non pay benefits would be most we well received are the people who would receive them. All too often organisations determine benefits with their accountant rather than with their cook!

Find the talent that someone else is discarding

I am afraid that a popular time of the year when pre-schools will close down, will be after October half term, in July, and following the Christmas break. These pre-schools may have become financially unviable despite the best efforts of their staff so don't feel they won't be where Superstars hang out. Superstars may be the talent that someone else is discarding. You may be approached by the Committee of such Pre- Schools looking to assist displaced staff. You could also approach them to see if they would be able to share your vacancies. Don't be embarrassed. As the saying goes, "Good Fortune Favours the Bold!"

Equally don't be afraid to follow up with local competitors who you discover are in trouble for one reason or another. Over the past years I've been working within the sector several providers in the West Midlands have found themselves closed due to one safeguarding reason or another.

Of course it's often the case that not *all* the staff in the Nursery will be to blame for these closures, and I've seen many Day Nurseries close in on displaced staff and offer them new opportunities. Some weren't even hiring at the time, but saw the opportunity to hire Superstars and didn't miss out.

Chapter 4

Crafting the Environment for a Superstar to work in

"If you do what you've always done, you'll get what you've always got."

Henry Ford

In order for a Superstar to perform they need an environment at work that will be congruent with their Superstar performance.

Therefore before you go to out to recruit your Superstar it may be a very good idea to cast an unbiased eye over the environment in which the new recruit will work in.

Before you hold interviews in the Nursery perhaps you want to look as to whether you are 'putting your best face on'. Is the Nursery a mess? Do you need to hire cleaners or are your staff maintaining the housekeeping well enough without the additional expense?

Superstar hires may have their own 'wish-list' for what they would want from their new employer. Commonly these include:

- Career progression.
- Work Life Balance – particularly opportunity for four day compressed hours week and Flexible Working opportunities.
- Short commutes.
- Well planned induction programme (See Chapter 19).
- Fair and consistent management practices.
- Subsidised or reduced childcare costs.
- Access to Continuous Professional Development (CPD)
- Competitive reward package.

If these are included in the offer, make sure that you spend time pointing these out to the Superstar candidate during the selection process. That's in the Application Pack, interview and any correspondence between you.

In terms of environment, in this Chapter we are going to look at the impact of the following aspects of the work environment and the positive and negative impacts they can have on a new hire:

- Technology.
- Facilities.
- Employment documentation.
- Training and Development.
- Communication channels.
- Uniforms & Branding.

Technology

Have you been thinking about introducing new technology into your Nursery, but not moved those plans along? A Superstar hire will have an understanding of what technology is used in outstanding settings and may well have an expectation that the advances would be available to staff at your Nursery. For example paper based learning journals. You have may always utilised the paper based approach; and there is absolutely nothing wrong with that approach, however with the recent emergence in online learning journals such as Tapestry, practitioners are seeing how useful they are and how flexible can be. Your Superstar candidate may ask you about the use of tablets in the setting and you may want to consider your response before they ask the question.

Additional questions to ask about technology are:

- Do your staff use an ancient PC that takes an age to 'boot up'? Do they have the facilities to print and scan? Can they access the internet? Can they use email?

Facilities

What are your staff facilities like? Do you provide somewhere for your staff to secure their belongings, such as a staff room or locker room? Can they park at/or near to your place of work? Is it free or does it cost? Do you provide security lighting for your staff and parents so they feel safe when they arrive in the dark winter mornings, or leave in the dark after securing your building? Do you have an area where staff can have their breaks? Is there a working fridge for them, a fruit bowl, free hot drinks and access to refreshing chilled water? Can your kitchen provide a hot meal for someone working a 10 hour shift?

Do you rooms smell of recent nappies changes? Is there a lovely smell coming from the kitchen of cookies being baked after being assembled by small hands?

Are you using the features of your building to best advantage? I visit some beautiful period buildings that have retained their period features. Some of them clearly use the natural environment as part of their ethos. Beautiful oak doors and sanded floors, even pre-loved Ercol dining tables that have been upcycled for use with the children. I've seen Mahogany display cabinets with glass removed for the children to display their makes. Everyone feels happier surrounded by beautiful things.

The environment is a big motivator for your staff.

Here's a big question to ask yourself is "Do your staff toilets lack love?"

You may think that is a strange question. But toilets are one of the most indicative areas of your Nursery. If your staff toilets are unhygienic, smelly and lacking in any love that speaks volumes about how you view your staff and their basic human needs.

I've visited some desirable Day Nurseries who have had some shocking toilets. Toilets that the staff share with the vacuum cleaner, mop buckets, cleaning products and no sanitary waste facilities. In 2016 it's just wrong!

I've also visited some Day Nurseries where for a few pounds the Owner has purchased an attractive fake flower arrangement, a bowl of lovely smellies, some luxurious hand cream, with air fresheners and some cheap but smart art on the wall. Those toilets are a pleasure to use and their staff feel appreciated by their employer.

Additional questions about your physical environment may include:

- Do you have a lot of hand written notices up, blu-tacked to the walls and doors? This can look messy and that you don't care. If you don't maintain the building or at least have a plan to do so, why would you staff get the Cif out and rub off that dirty mark they've just created on the wall?

Employment Documentation

When you've hired your Superstar you are going to issue them with a Written Statement of Terms and Conditions. It must give the right impression. A dodgy looking contract with suspicious looking clauses will cause the Superstar to question their decision to join you. All employees have a contract of employment, which forms the basis of the employment relationship. Apprentices and those on a Fixed Term contract should have their contracts specifically prepared for their circumstances. If someone is a term time only employee, they still need a contract of employment that reflects their term time only status.

The Employment Rights Act 1996 requires employers to issue employees with their Written Statement of Terms and Conditions within 8 weeks of an employee starting work.

The following details should be included in the written statement:

- The employee's name.
- The employer's name (this was highlighted as an issue in the serious case review of Vanessa George).
- The Job Title or a brief job description.
- The date employment began, the place of work and the address of employer.
- The amount of pay and intervals between payments.
- Hours of work.
- Holiday pay entitlement.
- Sick pay entitlement.
- Pension Arrangements.
- Notice Periods.
- Where the employment is not permanent, the period it is expected to continue.
- Where employment is fixed term, the date when it is to end.
- Disciplinary rules – or reference to the Disciplinary Procedure.
- Grievance rules - or reference to the Grievance Procedure.
- Whether any collective agreements exist that effect the terms and conditions.

- A declaration statement to be signed by the employee

Training & Development

What's your Training and Development Plan like? Do you invest in staff development and training? Do your staff realise it's an investment and that you investing in them is for both of your benefits.

If training is seen as mandatory and common place, it is hard for staff to be excited about it unless their previous setting made staff request training and then maintained minimum numbers of individuals trained. For example with paediatric First Aid until it becomes a requirement that all staff hold this training certificate, some settings will operate on the basis of the minimum number trained per floor/room. You offering this to all staff on the basis that it is considered to be best practice will stand you above the competition; who don't see this as mandatory.

Do you see attendance at seminars and workshops as being something only management do, or do you open these up to other staff? If spaces are limited a ballot can be a fair way of identifying who you will take. Everyone who would like to apply to go is put into a ballot and the lucky individuals will be one's whose names are pulled from the hat.

Do you recognise training achievement? You don't have to go to huge expense to publically recognise achievement and gratitude for a job done well. We often see photos on social media of employee's holding their certificates, these are well shared by the staff and their family members and it gives a very favourable impression of the Day Nursery.

Communication channels

We all know that communication is only effective if it is two way. Don't be bashful about the extent to which you have developed your effective communication channels.

If you don't have effective communication, how will your Superstar recognise what's needed and when.

Make sure that you are communicating that you use Appraisal and Supervision, that you have staff meetings and a Staff Newsletter. That they can take part in the social scene at the Nursery, whether that's cinema nights or bowling; make sure that these are communicated and that the Superstar candidate is very impressed by the amount of communication channels that exist.

Uniform

Will your Superstars, swell with pride when given the smart uniform you want them to wear or will they be embarrassed by that second hand sweater with a strange smell?

Uniform serves two purposes; it promotes your brand; the staff who wear it should feel proud of the brand they represent; and it should protect the employee's own clothes.

Wearing a uniform and being responsible for its laundry means that the staff member is under more pressure than someone who can wear anything so long as it's black and white.

Anyone who thinks it easier to have a uniform than not, is mistaken. Make sure you are proud of your uniform and if for any reason you decide to change the uniform make sure you consult with those staff who will wear it and involve them in the decision on what to wear next. Your staff will love you for it!

Do you provide coats, jackets, fleeces or waterproofs to encourage your staff to go out in all weathers with the children?

These can make a massive difference to the staff and mean your team are a walking advert when out with the children in the local community.

Chapter 5

Designing the Role

Designing the role is a multifaceted approach. You are looking at the description of the job to be performed, the job title and the roles and responsibilities that you document as part of the selection and future performance management of the hire.

Choosing a Job Title - Is the title compelling?

It's probably the first thing that the Superstar candidate will see that reflects the job. Long before they have read the job description or your advert they will see the title you have chosen for the post.

Think about why the right person will want this job. Currently it is common to call new appointments Early Years Educators rather than Nursery Nurses. Cleaners are often referred to as Housekeepers and Nursery Cooks are described as Nursery Chefs.

Think also about what will be searched on the internet by the Superstar looking for work? Will they be searching for Nursery Nurse rather than Early Years' Educator or Early Years Practitioner? No point having a title no one recognises.

Job Enrichment

The motivational theorist Frederick Hertzberg first wrote about job enrichment in 1968 in a paper about pioneering approaches at the large American firm AT&T.

Job enrichment is where management can motivate self-driven employees by assigning them responsibility normally reserved for senior management. An example of this may be appointing a Nursery Nurse as SEND Co-ordinator (after sending them on the appropriate training) because they showed an aptitude for this and wanted the additional responsibility at a time when there was no vacancy for a Deputy Manager at the setting.

Further examples of job enrichment in Early Years' that I have come across include:

- Training a Nursery Nurse to be a Manual Handling Techniques Trainer and thus able to train her colleagues in safe manual handling technique.
- Fire Wardens who are Nursery Assistants and Cooks.
- Health and Safety Officer who was also a Room Leader.

Enrichment is about additional responsibilities, aspects of the role that will stretch the individual to perform the role. Giving them a challenging role with the opportunity for them to enhance their skills will give the individual reason to stay and engage with you in the long term.

You need to design an enriching job role otherwise your selected Superstar will not stay.

Producing a Job Description

There is no better document to describe the job you want to fill than the job description. Over the years job descriptions have come in and out of fashion. Right now they are back in fashion in a big way and particularly useful in the Early Years' sector.

Not so long ago there was a general feeling that unless you wanted your staff to be able to say "it's not my job to do X, it's not in my job description!" then you didn't create and issue job descriptions.

The truth is **without** a job description you will never be able to manage performance.

Job Descriptions provide:

- A clear description of responsibilities for which an employee is held accountable.
- A reference for performance management and appraisal.
- Parameters of responsibility.
- A link to task management.
- A link to career progression and next steps.
- Clear expectations about behaviour.

Your job descriptions are your best friends, look after them and they will look after you.

If you don't use them, whoever you hire will never know what is expected of them in the role, they won't fully understand the contribution they are to make, and won't understand the responsibilities and scope of the role they are to perform. Basically it'll fail.

If you produce one for each post holder you can then sit down with someone and go through their job description at induction and ask them sign a copy for their personnel file. You will both know where you stand and what is expected, without it being left to guesswork.

Attractive job descriptions are a real bonus and will attract Superstars to your Day Nursery.

Just as for your job advert you can get a template from a designer on a site like upwork.com or fiverr.com at relatively little expense and if you have a number of documents with the same 'look' such as the advert, person specification and about the Nursery page, all the better. It shows you have taken some time and trouble over this stage of the employer/employee relationship and creates a good impression.

There are three main purposes of a Job Description:

1. To attract candidates to apply for the post. If written well your job description will bring the post alive to the reader, if they are interested they will 'see themselves' undertaking the role you have described in your setting.
2. Define the Role. The level of effort required to define the role will always pay you dividends.
3. Show the level of responsibility of the Manager. This aspect is incredibly important where you have other Managers, or an Owner involved in the Nursery. Imagine the chaos if a role doesn't

separate out who is responsible for what. I've known many a Manager to assume additional responsibility that wasn't theirs to have. I've also known Manager's 'disabled' by fear and underperform because they assume that an Owner will want to have responsibility for a certain task when in fact, the Owner expected that the Manager would be responsible for that task.

When preparing a Job Description we do see some common mistakes. These include:

1. Not proof reading the Job Description. If you are going to expect a good level of written English from the post holder you don't want the Job Description to show any lack of skill on your part. The key here is to find someone who is good at grammar, spelling etc. to proof read what you've produced.

2. Using lots of internal terminology. A good Job Description is written in plain English and whilst you would expect to see industry specific terminology less internal terminology is a very good idea. You know that Pippins is the name of the Pre-School room, but will a candidate?

3. Writing the Job Description in isolation. Write a job description with the help of colleagues. If introducing them for the first time, write it with the current job holder, their colleagues, and Managers. It shouldn't be one perspective and the work of one individual.

4. Being unrealistic with expectations. I've read very long Job Descriptions with very detailed

responsibilities and requirements of the job and then seen a very unrealistic salary. I've also seen full time posts described as 10 hours a day, Monday to Friday, 7.30 a.m. to 6.30 p.m. with an hour's unpaid lunch, 50 hours a week, for a Manager this is not conducive to effective performance.

The basic elements of a job description will be:

Job Title:

Responsible to:

Responsible for: (if no-one state not applicable or n/a)

Summary of role:

- Bulleted list describing the essential elements of the post.

And a final bullet that states 'any other task as deemed reasonable.'

Roles in Early Years' are constantly evolving and therefore Job Descriptions should not be left, un-reviewed for any length of time.

I recommend you review your Job Descriptions at least annually. Each Job Description should have an Issue Number, Issue Date and initials of the person who pulled it together. Never overwrite a Job Description when you update one, save the Job Description as a new file on your word processing software and keep the previous copy so you can show how the role was developed.

You may want to review your Job Descriptions:

1. At appraisal – as part of the appraisal interview it would be a good idea to review the individuals Job Description with them and ask them whether they feel it is a true reflection of their role in the organisation.

2. When Hiring – even for roles you hire for regularly, this opportunity for you to update the Job Description before you make your next appointment.

3. Following a Disciplinary – if you find yourself disciplining a staff member you may find it useful to update the Job Description. Always remember though that you shouldn't take responsibility off someone after a disciplinary unless it has been agreed as a better situation going forward. Allegations of constructive dismissal can arise from such situations, always take advice from a HR Consultant or similar before updating a Job Description in such circumstances.

Here is an example of a Job Description for the post of Nursery Cook.

Title: Nursery Cook

Responsible to: The Nursery Manager

Responsibility for: The Cook is responsible for the management of any temporary or permanent staff employed as kitchen assistants in the Nursery.

Purpose of the job:

To be responsible for the organisation and management of the kitchen/ serving area and to prepare healthy meals and snacks for children of the Day Nursery, in accordance with nutritional guidelines and policies and procedures.

Main duties:

- To prepare two cooked meals and two snacks per day for children of all ages in the centre, taking into account dietary requirements and allergy guidelines.

- To direct and supervise kitchen staff in their duties.

- To take responsibility for the safe storage and preparation of food, maintain high standards of cleanliness and food hygiene and complete appropriate records.

- To dispose of any out of date food,

- To plan weekly menus that provide healthy, nutritionally balanced meals for young children.

- To manage the ordering of food from approved suppliers taking account of quality, seasonality and affordability, and complete appropriate daily and weekly records.

- To minimise wastage.

- To ensure all equipment is in good working order, reporting any breakages, issues to Nursery Manager and to complete daily and weekly cleaning records.

- To minimise fire risks and ensure fire equipment is well maintained.

- To conform to Health and Safety regulations at all times.

- To prevent entry to the kitchen by non-authorised personnel.

- To undertake a stock take as required.

- To maintain standards in the kitchen by undertaking preventative and reactive cleaning activities including 'deep cleans' as required.

- To maintain up-to-date food hygiene qualifications.

- To support the nursery in the attainment of Healthy Eating Award.

- Any other duties as deemed reasonable.

Chapter 6

Deciding on Your Superstar's Behaviours

"Hire for Attitude; Train for Skill"

Peter Schultz

Once you have decided on the role and prepared the Job Description, you can set about deciding on what type of person you will want to fill your vacancy and you can prepare the Person Specification.

There's no doubt that it takes effort to produce a Person Specification. A Person Specification describes the person you are seeking for the role. It's as useful to the Nursery as the Job Description is and can lead to you avoiding costly hiring mistakes.

Producing a Person Specification that you share with candidates in the Candidate Information Pack sends out the message that you care that the position is successfully filled. The Superstar will be more inclined to apply for the position within an organisation that has taken the time to define who they are looking to fill their vacancy.

A Person Specification also reduces the chance that your advert will be discriminatory. By defining what you seek, before a single candidate applies, it means you can avoid allegations that you have not offered the job to a specific candidate. Here's an example of this in action.

A Nursery has a rural location without good transport links. It realises that its location impacts the people it employs and when preparing the Person Specification it includes as an essential criteria that post holder will have their own transport.

A candidate applies and that states on their application that they would use public transport to get to a job. As the employer knows the nearest bus stop is one mile away, the employer determines not to interview the candidate. The candidate complains that they rejected her application unfairly. The employer can then refer the candidate to the pre-produced Person Specification and demonstrate where the candidate failed to meet an essential criterion. This results in the complaint being dropped.

A Person Specification will typically include:

- The qualifications and competencies required for the post.
- Experience/achievements.
- Skills required.
- Competencies regards to complete the job to a high standard.
- Abilities involved in working with a team.
- Expected breadth and depth of experience.
- Personal attributes and circumstances. i.e. the ability to work between 7.30 a.m. and 6 p.m. would be useful for Day Nurseries.

A Person Specification has limited use in the employment cycle, because unlike a competency framework it doesn't have much use outside of selection. A competency framework can be used for selection, induction and in some cases exit (through redundancy).

The Person Specification will describe the experience, qualifications, skills, and attributes of the successful candidate.

Using it will reduce any opportunity for someone to allege that you have discriminated by not offering them the position and you should be able to show that you have hired the **best** person to fill the vacancy based on the person specification you prepared before you had met the first candidate.

All criteria you use should:

- Be non-discriminatory
- Be linked to the role.

Person Specifications often follow one of two plans, either Rodger's Seven Point Plan or Munro Fraser's Five Point Plan.

Rodger's Seven Point Plan is made up of:

1. Physical make-up health, physique, appearance, bearing and speech
2. Attainments education, qualifications, experience.
3. General intelligence fundamental intellectual capacity.

4. Special aptitudes mechanical, manual dexterity, computer literacy, etc.
5. Interests intellectual, practical –constructional, physically, active, social, artistic
6. Disposition acceptability, influence over others, steadiness, dependability, self-reliance.
7. Circumstances, i.e. flexibility, driving licence.

Munro Fraser's Five Point Grading System includes:

1. Impact on others – physical make-up, speech, and manner.
2. Acquired qualifications – education, vocational training, and work experience.
3. Innate abilities – natural quickness of comprehension and aptitude for learning.
4. Motivation – kind of goals set by the individual, his/her consistency and determination in following them up, his/her success in achieving them.
5. Adjustment –emotional stability, ability to stand up to stress, ability to get on with people.

Naturally, I prefer the Edmunds' Five Point Person Specification which is made up of:

1. Education, qualifications and courses.
2. Situation, previous experience, background training and availability.
3. Attitude; i.e. preparedness to continue professional development.
4. Aptitudes, these are the abilities not adequately described by the possession of qualification, such

as Sense of Humour, Ability to Work with Others etc.

5.   Circumstances, i.e. able to work shifts, own transport, flexible as to hours worked etc.

You don't have to any of these plans you can choose your own and produce your own Person Specification template.

Once you have identified the elements of the person specification; you need to determine whether achieving this element is essential, desirable or a disqualifier. The key to success here is to 'get off the fence'. If you want the element to be essential state that it must be essential, if everything is desirable you will find the effectiveness of the Person Specification reduced as you will not be able to determine between candidates.

Here's an extract of a Person Specification for a Nursery Nurse to explain my point.

Criteria	Essential	Desirable
Qualifications	Possesses an NVQ Level 3 in Childcare or equivalent.	An NVQ Level 4 or above qualification in Childcare or equivalent.

Here the employer is describing what he/she would consider the essential requirement for the post and what he/she would describe as desirable. Therefore if they have candidates with higher than NVQ Level 3 qualifications, they may determine to interview those at a preference to those who meet the essential requirement of a NVQ Level

3. Any candidate who possesses a NVQ Level 2 will go no further in the process.

Note that the employer is requiring that the candidate demonstrates or evidences the qualifications. Sadly some people will lie about qualifications, or will be unclear as to what qualifications they have. I can recall an individual in the sector who applied stating they have a NVQ Level 3, when in reality they had units *towards* an NVQ Level 3. Make sure you see the original certificates at interview and take copies of them for your personnel files. Annotate that original certificates were seen and the date. If in any doubt as to the validity of the certificate check with the issuer who should be able to verify that the certificate is a genuine one for you.

To check the equivalency of qualifications use the National Recognition Information Centre (NARIC). This allows you to compare foreign qualifications.

The access the process visit www.naric.org.uk

An example of a Person Specification for a Nursery Cook is as follows:

Criteria	Essential	Desirable
Qualifications	<ul><li>C&G or NVQ L3 catering</li><li>Food Hygiene Certificate</li></ul>	<ul><li>Level 3 or above qualification in Childcare, Health and Safety, or Supervision.</li></ul>
Situation	<ul><li>Awareness of nutritional guidelines for children under five.</li><li>Working knowledge of the Health and Safety at Work Act 1974 and Management of Safety Regulations (6 Pack)</li></ul>	<ul><li>Experience of team working in a kitchen.</li><li>Experience of stock control, managing budgets, working with suppliers.</li></ul>
Attitude	<ul><li>Positive attitude towards healthy eating.</li><li>Awareness of Equal opportunities and promoting inclusiveness in a Day Nursery.</li><li>Able to work to budget.</li></ul>	<ul><li></li></ul>
Aptitude	<ul><li>Friendly and Approachable</li><li>Likes working with children.</li><li>Team Player</li><li>'Can Do' Attitude</li><li>Able to organise others.</li><li>Time Management Skills.</li></ul>	<ul><li>Preparedness to attend training.</li></ul>
Circumstances	<ul><li>Member of Update Service</li><li>Able to work flexible hours to meet the needs of the Nursery.</li><li>Full UK Driving licence.</li></ul>	<ul><li>Prepared to apply for enhanced DBS</li></ul>

Chapter 7

Designing the Advert

Once you have designed the job description and identified the behaviours you seek from the ideal post holder you can think about designing your advert.

Write to the ideal candidate

In the advert you should be writing to the Superstar you seek. Think about them being sat alongside you on a park bench and you are telling them about the position you seek to fill.

You are trying to write a personal message to the ideal person you wish to hire, therefore try picturing this person reading your advert.

Do people know who you are?

If you are a local branch of a national chain of nurseries, there's a good chance that the candidate will have heard of your business and will be familiar with the name. If that's the case you could argue that you don't need to take up valuable space on the advert describing your setting.

If you are not well known or may be sharing your advert outside of your local environment you should set aside a section of the advert to describing your setting and what you offer.

This could be a paragraph from your websites' Home page or a section of your prospectus.

If you have Ofsted Outstanding, why not use the image in the advert.

Don't be tempted to describe your setting as offering outstanding level of care if you are not an Ofsted Outstanding setting. This creates a bad impression with the candidate and just looks naff!

Use words to describe your setting that are descriptive without suggesting that you are indirectly discriminatory. See later in this Chapter. Care should be taken when describing the team as young and dynamic, as this can give the impression that you are not looking for an older candidate to fit in with the team. The word mature should also be avoided. We all know that you can be mature in attitude as well as years, but to include it will give someone the impression that a younger candidate should not apply. This can also be alleged to be age discriminatory, remember age discrimination is not an older person's issue in isolation.

Is it clear where you are?

Many adverts in local papers rely on the reader having recognition of the setting and being familiar as to where the setting is located. Online it's important to make sure that candidates know where you are. Include an address in the advert drawing the candidate's attention to any known issues around the location using phrases such as rural location, or that own transport is necessary due to rural location. It would be discriminatory to state in the advert that a car driver is required due to rural location if in fact the candidate could use moped, motorbike, bike, to get to the setting. You can only ask for a car driver if driving will be required to perform the role.

Are you able to offer a relocation bonus?

If you are attracting a Superstar who is in the position to relocate to your local area to take the position you may want to consider offering a relocation bonus for the right candidate.

Imagine a Superstar who is a female in her late 20's who is single and currently rents a home. Her expenses to move will often include the cost of renting a new home with a letting agent. They typically charge prospective tenants for searches and the registration of them as a new tenant. This can go into the hundreds of pounds.

If you offer a £500 relocation bonus this could attract a Superstar to your setting that is looking to base themselves in your locality. If someone is willing to do that for the right position can you make it easier for them?

Safeguarding statement

Include a statement that the setting is committed to safeguarding and promoting the welfare of children by checking references and that the position is subject to an enhanced Disclosure and Barring Service check. In the current Statutory Framework for the Early Years Foundation Stage, paragraph 3.11 states;

"Providers must tell staff that they are expected to disclose any convictions, cautions, court orders, reprimands and warnings that may affect their suitability to work with children (whether received before or during their employment at the setting). Providers must not allow people whose suitability has not been checked including through a criminal records check to have unsupervised contact for children being cared for."

The Superstar candidate will expect to see a safeguarding statement and it could concern them about your adherence with the EYFS if you do not.

Childcare employers have an exemption from the Rehabilitation of Offenders Act because spent convictions must be revealed. If you would like to a statement that you are an Equal Opportunities employer can be included. However as an Early Years' employer you do have an exemption under the Rehabilitation of Offenders Act, therefore I would suggest that stating you are an Equal Opportunities employer is a little disingenuous.

Salary information in the advert

I am a firm believer that you should include a salary or hourly rate (as applicable) in your advert. It prevents time being wasted by you or the candidate. Your Superstars are looking for the transparency that comes with an employer stating the salary in the advert. No one really appreciates the term £competitive or £excellent plus benefits. If it is so competitive why are you not shouting it from the rooftops! If you are genuinely unsure as to the exact salary you will offer, because it may differ depending on experience and qualifications that the ideal candidate may bring, you can use a phrase such as circa.£19k, as an alternative to not including the information.

How to apply?

With your advert you should make it clear how you would like your candidate to apply for your vacancy.

If you would like the candidate to print off the application form from your website you should direct the candidate in the advert as to where this can be found. If you web address (the url) is too long why not consider shortening it with the site www.bit.ly.com where you can; for free, shorten a long web address into a shorter one. If you create a free account within the website you can track the number of 'hits' that you get on this address. This can help prove the quality of the advert (or not) or the effectiveness of the method of advertising. This is an ideal tracking method to measure the effectiveness of the chosen method of advertising.

Alternatively, if you feel your candidate will be local, you may advise that applications are available from the Office or Reception. This suggestion in the advert may put off candidates who feel that they cannot easily visit you to collect an application form during your opening hours.

If you are using a Candidate Information Pack (and I would recommend you do) these can be pre-produced and ready to be handed out or posted to interested candidates. Alternatively can they be downloaded from your setting's website. If you have packs I would recommend they are saved as Adobe PDF files so that the content cannot be changed by the candidate.

If you decide to allow candidates to apply initially with a CV you may want candidates to email you their CV to a specific address. I would recommend if you choose to do this that you include a unnamed address such as jobs@ or careers@ rather than sue.smith@ as there is a risk that the email address will be harvested by recruitment agencies and similar who will make speculative approaches. The benefit of the CV first approach from the perspective of the candidate is that it is quick and easy. A Superstar doesn't necessarily only do what is quick and easy! I feel that for the purposes of Safer Recruitment, completing an application form is a much more robust approach to recruitment than submitting a CV.

Can candidates initially get in touch for an informal chat?

The benefit of inviting candidates to initially contact the employer for an informal chat is definitely valuable for certain roles. In particular role such as Operations Manager, Nursery Manager or Pre School Leader the candidate could approach a Director, Owner or Chair of Pre School for an informal chat before applying. The Superstar candidate may want to have an informal chat just to discover more about the vacancy, the expectations of the employer, the reason the vacancy has become available and such like. The offer may never be picked up by candidates but I do think it speaks volumes of your personality as an employer and your preparedness to support the Superstar candidate. After an informal chat, both parties may recognise that it would not be worthwhile taking an application forward, and for the cost of the call, time and effort has not been wasted. Always check what telephone number they would want to be approached on and I would recommend that this number is pre-registered with the Telephone Preference Service (TPS) in case anyone picks up this number and decides to use it for marketing purposes. Additionally if there are only certain times when the individual is available state the hours on the advert. This prevents embarrassment and may encourage someone to call.

When to apply and deadlines

Adverts in papers and magazines will often hang around longer than online adverts that may be limited in their publication. It's important if you have a deadline for applications to include this in the advert, particularly if you are going to print.

The first consideration is: When will the publication be available? Probably much later than the deadline for the advert you have been given by the Advertising Dept. There is no point having a paper available for candidates on a Friday evening with a deadline of a Monday, giving candidates very little time to make their effective application.

Having a deadline also creates a 'call to action'. Apply by. This is telling the candidate that if this position is attractive to you; we need your application by this date. If we receive the application late, it will be **too** late. In our busy lives we often need a 'call to action' if we are to take immediate action. You will want your Superstar to take action and get their application in. A deadline then is a very good idea. If you have an idea as to when you will be interviewing candidates you have a couple of choices. You can include a statement such as 'interviews will take place in week commencing [insert date] or say when interviews will take place. I recommend a week commencing approach as life has an awkward way of getting in the way of plans at times. If you have stated interviews are on a particular date and you need to move it you may appear disorganised or even face the allegation that X would have applied if they had known that interviews were not going to be held on [date]. Remember some candidates will look at your date and realise they can't be available and therefore not apply. Be flexible, in real terms you may be able to interview candidates at 6.30 p.m. or on a Saturday morning, to make sure you see the ideal candidate. A Superstar won't want to let down their current employer in order to attend your interview.

Treat the candidate like a VIP customer

Whilst you are trying to attract the candidate to a position within your setting, treating them like a VIP customer is a great way to ensure that you make people feel welcome. All too often I see candidates, good candidates treated with disdain and people wonder why they struggle to recruit. When you spot what you are looking for move quickly, as Superstars will be off looking elsewhere.

Chapter 8

Where do Superstar's Hang Out

If you want a Superstar to apply you need to think about where Superstars hangout in numbers.

Superstars may not be looking for work, when they are performing a role competently and well for someone else.

Your Superstar candidates may be browsing social media, chatting with friends over a coffee, flicking through a local paper when they come across your advertisement.

Out of our friends and contacts, each of us probably has 250 people who we could have a conversation with. That's a lot of people. Your staff will each have 250 people, so a Day Nursery of 20 staff could give you access to 5000 people to be told about your vacancy. (Yes, I do realise you're not going to want to have that many conversations!)

Word of Mouth

As an informal approach to recruitment this one is as old as the hills! It's effective though and if you have a notice board why not advertise your vacancies internally giving your team heads up about vacancies you have to fill.

When your staff know that you are looking to fill a vacancy they may share with people in their network that you are hiring. As people know people like themselves, if you currently employ Superstars, they will know other Superstars and some of them may also be Early Years qualified! The notice may be seen by your Improvement Advisors, Trainers and Consultants who all visit your setting.

The downside of word of mouth is that we tend to know people like us and this can lead to accusations of perpetuating the workforce. To give you an example if you workforce is made up of women between the age of 25-30, the majority of the people in their network, will be women aged 25-30. This approach may not help to appoint an older male employee for example.

Can you incentivise?

Many employers incentivise their existing staff to help them recruit new people by introducing an Employee Referral Scheme. These forms of incentive can be very effective but they come with a few cautionary observations:

Recruiting people known to your existing staff may mean:

- Recruiting members of the same family (can be problematic).
- Recruiting individuals who are in friendships with your existing staff (can be problematic).
- Negatively impact equal opportunities.
- Impact diversity and the benefits the Day Nursery gains having a diverse workforce.

If you want to introduce an Employee Referral Scheme you should ensure that any payment you give is split so an amount is paid if the referral is hired, and a further amount if they complete the probationary period.

You may also think about rewarding both the candidate and the referrer. This works in much the same way as the telecommunications companies who approach their marketing by rewarding the customer for referring a new customer by giving the same reward to both the existing and new customer for the referral.

The benefit of this approach is that there is something for both parties, which can support the friendship as no one is seen to profit from the connection. The other benefit is that if payments are split, it may encourage the performance from the new employee in the probationary period. The downside is that it may cost you more to run such an incentive than it would do if you just rewarded the existing employee.

Make sure the scheme is open to all and keep the payment simple. The more complicated you make the scheme the less likely your staff are going to not bother with it. Likewise no one is going to put their reputation on the line for a tenner.

Get on Facebook

The first thing you must do if you want to use Facebook to advertise your vacancies is to get a Facebook page for your Nursery. This is not a personal page but a business or a community page if you are a 'not for profit' setting. You should have two administrators who can access the page to make changes from their personal Facebook login account.

Don't worry no one will be able to see their personal account and their privacy will be maintained.

Once you have set up a Facebook page you can start posting to groups and other pages about your vacancies, as well as sharing the vacancy with individuals who have liked your page.

Facebook is a business and as such you can use paid for advertising to get your vacancy advert in front of your target audience. The level of information Facebook has about its users is very detailed and gets more detailed every week. It's one of the reasons some people are very uncomfortable about social media, and in particular Facebook.

For example you will be able to target women between the age of 25-40, living in your town, who like the National Day Nursery Association.

In my opinion this is both amazing and scary at the same time! Facebook advertising is relatively low cost (compared to print or Linkedin Advertising) and you can set a budget for the campaign.

After you've established your page you can encourage parents, staff and friends to like your page. Ask them to spread the word so you are reaching a larger network.

Put a link to your Facebook page on your website. In both the adverts you post to your page and your page itself what you stand for as a Nursery should stand out. Superstars want to work for a Nursery that shares the same values and beliefs as they do, you will communicate your values in many ways from pictures, memes, the quotes you choose, the pages you share, to the posts you make about your setting and your team.

Some posts don't belong on your Facebook page, like telling the parents off. We see this surprisingly often, along with comments from readers, such as "I don't use your Nursery and I will not be doing so if that's how you speak to your parents!"

A Facebook page that thanks its staff for the wonderful experience they provide the children each and every day does send out the signal that staff are valued and appreciated. You may consider using your Facebook page to show off your Employee of the Month or similar employee reward system.

If you are going to use images of your staff on your Facebook page you must have a Model Release Form signed and on their personnel file.

You should also direct Facebook visitors back to your website where more information can be found about the Nursery and your values and beliefs.

When posting a vacancy on Facebook you have to be prepared to post regularly. Within Facebook you can schedule posts and this will allow you to have a post coming out a time of day when your audience is most likely to be on line. If you think about it your Superstar is likely only to be on line during their lunchbreak and after work Monday to Friday. There would seem little point posting at 9.30 a.m. The website, Hootsuite.com allows you to pre-schedule multiple posts of the same advert, so you don't have to remember to do it daily. It takes many posts to fill a vacancy.

If you prefer you can link your Facebook post to your online advert on jobs boards such as www.indeed.com, that way your applicants are going to Indeed for more information about your vacancy rather than back to your website. If you web designer is outsourced this may be a cheaper option than asking for updated of your website each time you have a vacancy to fill.

Using Facebook to advertise vacancies does take time, as I have said before, having a template and using it to share your vacancy will increase the potential that you will find your Superstar on line.

New Facebook groups are being launched each week. A group differs from a page as the individual has asked to 'join' a group and will receive notification of every post that Group sends out. I would recommend using the Facebook group "Vacancies within the Early Years Sector" which, at the time of writing, has 3,200 subscribers.

Using Linkedin

Linkedin.com is another social media platform like Facebook. Linkedin attracts professionals so is unlikely to appeal as a platform to a Superstar Nursery Assistant but may be useful when recruiting a Nursery Manager or another senior management position.

Linkedin advertising is expensive. You could use your Linkedin profile to 'share' with connections that you are hiring. There are also Linkedin Groups in the same way there are Facebook groups. A Linkedin Group post appears in the individuals email inbox which we know to be very powerful in terms of engaging with candidates.

You should not 'spam' groups, (you will be asked to leave) but no one will be offended by you sharing your vacancies on Linkedin. You never know who may see the vacancy and be motivated to apply. Remember a Superstar is currently competently performing for someone else, so may not be active in their job search. With Linkedin you can catch them when they are 'just looking'.

I would recommend the Linkedin Group Passionate about Early Years as one to request to join.

Local Family Information Service

Your local Family Information Service (FIS) may have the facility to advertise your vacancies for your setting. They can have a section on their website or actually circulate vacancies to those on their 'list'. This is normally a free service.

Job Centre Plus

Advertising a vacancy with the Job Centre Plus may be useful to your setting. As well as helpful in attracting candidates it will also enable you to demonstrate your social responsibility as an employer. Employers who use advertising know that not everyone will be able to see the advert, so they place an advert on Job Centre Plus to prove their social responsibility. Any advert you place via the Government portal will also be displayed in local Job Centre Plus offices.

Could an Agency help?

A specialist recruitment agency may be useful to help find your Superstar who may have registered their CV with an agency.

Specialist recruitment agencies include:

- www.earlyyearsrecruitment.co.uk
- www.tinies.com
- www.eyears.co.uk
- Bamboochildcare
- Jemrecruitment.co.uk

Useful job websites include:

- Indeed.co.uk
- Nurseryworldjobs.co.uk

Chapter 9

Getting a Superstar to Apply

Once you have designed the role you are going to need to get the Superstar to apply.

Your Superstar will very often be working for someone else when they see your vacancy. Your role is to encourage them to 'get off their bum' and apply for your vacancy.

When someone is unemployed they may have a different strategy towards seeking a new opportunity, in fact they may be in a desperate race to find the next employment before they run out of cash! When someone is happy in their role but open to new challenges, you need to attract them to you and what you have to offer.

The top reasons people leave jobs they are performing well include;

- Prestigious opportunity i.e. the resources of the setting, brand name, outstanding accreditation, visionary leader etc.
- Less commute, no one likes long commutes to work and if someone has moved during their employment they may find that the commute is no longer any fun.
- Concerns over future of organisation. Good people leave organisations that they feel may be on the

wrong track. No one wants to be last off a sinking ship and good people may 'jump' before 'pushed'.

Advertising Vacancies

There is no general legal requirement to advertise your vacancies. The exception to this is that individuals employed on fixed term and part time contracts have the right to know about permanent positions in posts doing what they are employed to do.   To comply with this requirement we recommend you advertise internal vacancies within the organisation and encourage applicants from within the existing workforce.

You may decide to appoint without advertisement. Whilst there may be no legal requirement, there could be argued that there is a moral argument, and I would say that it has been proven to me over the years to make it very difficult for a candidate to be successful if internal candidates were not given the opportunity to put their proverbial 'hat in the ring'.

You need them to find out about your vacancy.

Options that are popular with Day Nurseries include:

- Advertising on Social Media, such as Facebook or Twitter.
- Advertising on Local Authority Early Years pages.
- On line advertising on Jobs Boards such as Indeed.com, Total Jobs, Reed.
- Advertising on Nursery World's website.
- Advertising from the Day Nurseries website.

- Advertising in local papers.
- Advertising in local supermarkets, post offices, local parish notice boards.
- Advertising by means of a physical banner outside the Day Nursery.

Superstars will be attracted to advertisements that show that the employer is going to nurture and recognise them. The language you use will be important to attract the Superstar.

It is important that you consider how you reflect the fact that positions in the Day Nursery will be exempt from the Rehabilitation of Offenders Act. You will want your staff to achieve an Enhanced Disclosure from the DBS that meets your requirements. You do not to attract inappropriate, unsuitable people to your Day Nursery.

An Example Disclaimer

Due to this post having access to children and/or vulnerable adults, candidates will be required to undertake a Disclosure and Barring Service check. The possession of a criminal record will not necessarily prevent an applicant from obtaining this post, as all cases are judged individually according to the nature of the role and information provided.

[insert organisation name] are committed to safeguarding and promoting the welfare of children and young people and expect all staff and volunteers to share this commitment.

Video

Can you produce a video for your website or your Facebook page introducing the vacancy?

Videos are very popular when they appear on social media timelines and are easy for individuals to share. Videos have greater organic reach on social media than images or just words. Organic reach is the number of people who can see your advert without you paying for the post. A video that gets its point across may only be one minute long and need not cost a lot of money to produce. I would recommend the website www.animoto.com as a means to produce a simple image based video with sound. There are some great examples of quirky videos on You Tube that have been used for advertising vacancies.

Produce an image to support your advert

We know that text based social media posts do not have the same organic (not paid for) reach of those that have an image.

Organic reach is important as it means that only around 15% of your page likes will see your post on their time line. When it is seen you want the settings of the post set so it can be shared easily and you want to interrupt the reader and for them to read your post in full. A picture can do that.

After all as they saying goes a picture paints a thousand words!

Some Day Nurseries have shown a real skill and expertise in commissioning eye catching adverts for use on social media.

In Figure 2 is an example from the Natural Childcare Company, shared with kind permission of their Director, Katie Landreth.

A DIY method would be to use Microsoft PowerPoint to design an advert that is then saved as a jpg file and uploaded to Facebook.

Figure 2

Using Free jobs boards

Increasingly employers in the sector will use free jobs boards on the internet to advertise their vacancies. A popular choice is the job board www.indeed.co.uk.

It is free to set up an account with indeed.co.uk and I would recommend you do so, even before you have a vacancy.

It is useful to research what other people are doing in your local area. Put in a job title and your town and you will see applicable searches. May be your competitor is expanding, may be you will learn the number of children registered at your local Pre-school has increased.

Whilst it can be used by employers for free, I would recommend using the Indeed sponsoring service, which is inexpensive and means your vacancy will 'stand head and shoulders' above other vacancies in the sector, advertised at the same time as yours.

At the time of writing this chapter, there were 186 vacancies for Nursery Nurses advertised on the site nationwide.

A few tips when using Indeed.co.uk

1. Use a job title that others will use in their search. Phrases like Nursery Nurse are more popular than Early Years' Practitioner.
2. Prepare a profile about your Day Nursery that will attract a Superstar. This may be the first that the

candidate sees about your Nursery. Make sure you leave a favourable impression.

3. Make the text easy to read by formatting it into paragraphs. Use bullets to both emphasise requirements and help the reader to absorb information. One long paragraph says you didn't try very hard.

4. Encourage candidates to follow your Day Nursery on social media and find out when you list other vacancies in the future. By following you they receive notifications in their emails. Good for you and them.

5. Use the reviews feature, to say what you are like as an employer.

6. Use photographs to show the location of your Nursery. This is especially useful if your front has what the designers describe as 'curb appeal'. Don't use photographs of the children or staff without expressed consent as to where the images can be used.

7. Mention the job title more than once in the copy to ensure it ranks well in search engine optimisation (SEO).

Indeed.co.uk gives the employer the ability to respond to applicants directly from the indeed portal. This is a very useful feature. Unfortunately candidates will apply by CV and as we described in another chapter this is not as desirable as an application form.

Chapter 10

Application Form or CV

Once you have designed the job, and identified the person who will be successful in this role, you need to consider how you would want them to apply for the position. Many employers require the candidate to apply via application form that the candidate either downloads from the website, or collects from Reception. Despite it being considered not part of Safer Recruitment many providers still ask the candidate to send them a CV.

If you use Application Forms it will give the right impression of your Day Nursery to Superstars and deter unsuitable or inappropriate people from applying who will be wasting their time and yours.

To be efficient with your money I would always advocate having the entire Application Pack available for download from your website or allowing candidates to collect from your reception. If you start posting application packs out to candidates you will see your recruitment costs rise and the quality of those who submit an application may not be as good.

An Application Form is a far better solution to the CV as the CV is often an exercise in creative writing. In my experience individuals may be more creative with the truth on a CV than they would be on an application form.

Using a standard application form for all positions that you advertise in the setting enables a range of important information to be collected in a systematic way. I would recommend a version of the application form is created for internal applications, for exactly the same reasons. Having an application form simplifies the entire shortlisting process. The shortlisting manager can compare 'apples with apples' rather than 'apples with oranges'. Applications can be quickly scanned to see whether the essential criteria of the person specification have been achieved. There are many risks for an employer using an application form, particularly if that form hasn't been updated since the introduction of the Equality Act in 2010.

Here's a list of some do's and don'ts with your application forms.

Do's

- Include your contact details and who the application should be sent to.
- A logo and any branding that your setting uses.
- Ask about previous paid and unpaid employment. Have dates so you can see any gaps in employment and ask the candidate about these at interview.
- Details of the contact information for the candidate including mobile phone number and email address.
- Whether they have any close family members who are employees at the setting or are parents of children who attend the setting.

- A question about whether they need any adjustment in order to participate with the selection process as a person who is considered disabled under the Equality Act 2010.
- A statement confirming that they know of no reason why an enhanced declaration from the Disclosure and Barring Service can't be obtained that is to the satisfaction of the employer.
- A signed statement confirming they are free from restriction to accept the employment.

Don'ts

- Ask whether they are registered disabled.
- Ask about the amount of time off they have had through sickness absence.
- Ask whether they are a disabled person under the Equality Act 2010.
- Ask them to complete equal opportunity information that is integrated into the application form.
- Whether the candidate drives unless it is an essential criterion of the post to have a driving licence.

Some candidates may need assistance to complete an Application Form. They may not be able to write in English. This may not be an essential or desirable criteria for the post and therefore it would be unfair for you to insist that the candidate completes their Application Form themselves. Always make sure you think about the candidate and if they need assistance offer it.

There are a number of "urban myths" around Application Forms. You are entitled to ask for a full name and whether the candidate can demonstrate their right to work in the UK. That is not discriminatory. You can also ask their date of birth so long that if challenged you can prove that the short-listers didn't use such information to age discriminate. It is important to know whether you are hiring someone who is below 18 as this will mean they will be treated as a young worker in employment law and entitled to different breaks than someone who is over 18 years of age. It can also affect the employer's ability to insure the employee to drive a Company owned vehicle. For example, if vehicle insurance was disproportionately higher for younger employees, it may be considered an 'objective justification' to not employ the younger candidate. Always take advice on matters that could give rise to claims of discrimination.

An application form can be used to:

- Establish full contact details including names known by.
- Establish qualifications;, be careful here as candidate often think they are NVQ qualified when in reality they have done an introductory course or part units towards a full NVQ.
- Invite candidates to give you more information as to why they feel they are suited to your position, you can always ask them to continue on a separate sheet if they like.

- Inform the candidate that the post is exempt from the provisions of the Rehabilitation of Offenders Act 1974.
- Request the details of references (See Chapter 17)

Possessing an Application Form makes it more effort for your candidate to apply to you, but you want to hire Superstars who are prepared to make an effort, not lazy people who feel you should accept their CV without an application form.

Ask for your application form to be completed in Black and in Block Capitals and see how many return one in blue and in lowercase. What does that tell you about their ability to follow instructions, it may be relevant?

Saying that; your application form should ideally be no more than four page long. It's important that your application form should be easy for the candidates to complete.

I find that having an application form on the website encourages candidate to complete the form, if they make a mistake, they can always print another!

Your web designer should be able to help you place a pdf of your application form on the website, if not you can find an individual with these web developer skills for little cost on www.upwork.com or www.fiverr.com

Chapter 11

Shortlisting Candidates to Interview

Understanding Your Responsibilities

When it comes to shortlisting candidates for interview, the employer is responsible to make sure they do not discriminate.

As you will be aware the employment legislation that covers discrimination is the Equality Act 2010.

Under the Equality Act 2010 is unlawful for discrimination to occur because of a 'protected characteristic'. There are currently 9 protected characteristics:

1. Age
2. Disability
3. Race
4. Religion & Beliefs
5. Sex
6. Sexual Orientation
7. Gender Reassignment
8. Marital Status
9. Pregnancy

I encourage short-listers to be trained in recruitment and selection and to be aware of the assumptions people often make when shortlisting candidates. I have known employers to estimate age on the basis of titles of examinations; to believe than an older candidate will be more loyal, committed and less likely to take time off. As we all know, the reality can be very different.

How to Shortlist

Hopefully you will be starting with a 'long list'. If your recruitment activity has been effective for you, you will have attracted a number of candidates of varying suitability. Your decision now is who to bring in for an interview so you can get to know the candidate and see how they would fit into your team. You should make sure you can shortlist in an environment which is peaceful and free from distraction. In front of you should be the job description, person specification and application forms. You will want some kind of candidate assessment sheet to identify which candidates have which criteria you were looking for when you advertised the post.

It is most likely that at the end of the short listing you will have three piles of applications. One that is marked 'Yes', one marked 'No', one marked 'Maybe'.

This is normal. If you have insufficient candidates in the Yes pile, consider whether any in the Maybe could be promoted to the 'Yes' pile. You should be consistent though. If you determine that candidates who do not have an essential criteria should be promoted to the Yes pile, then all the candidates who do not have that essential criteria should be promoted. At the same time, ask yourself whether the candidate who does not have an essential criteria; whether they have any chance of being successful in the role. Interviews are expensive to attend and run and it would be unfair to shortlist someone who you do not see as having a good chance of being successful.

Short Listing Panels

Some employers choose to form short listing panels that get together for the purpose of shortlisting which candidates will be invited for interview. The benefit of a shortlisting panel is that it is not one person's view, and therefore there would be less likelihood of bias. The downside of a short listing panel would be the time involved and the indirect cost of others being involved in the process at this stage. Panels typically have three members.

What if the candidates seek a job share?

From time to time, given the nature of the sector, we will receive candidates for full time jobs who are seeking a job share. This raises interesting questions for employers who may not have considered a job share until it is suggested by the candidate.

Let's make this clear, the employer is under no obligation to make the post a job share, and candidates who ask for a job share to be considered will often indicate who the other half of the share could be. If they do not, the employer is not expected to re-advertise for another half. Before you reject it as out of hand, I would ask yourself, what benefits could the organisation gain from a job share? What disadvantages are there that would overshadow these benefits? There is no doubt that job shares can be incredibly successful. Two part timers may be more flexible, more than capable of co-ordinating effectively between them without the need for a formal overlap. Additionally their mix of skills, interests and talents, may make them an enviable combination. I have known two teachers to take a Year 5 class, without the children being negatively impacted. They were best friends as well as job shares and communicated outside of the school really effectively. Without the job share, neither candidate would have been able to remain in teaching. Therefore the school's openness to the share was advantageous to the school, the individuals and the sector as a whole.

Notifying Applicants

Once you have shortlisted the candidates you should communicate your decision on their application.

Those who you have rejected at this stage should be informed in writing that their application has been unsuccessful. I would suggest that it is reasonable for such candidates to receive at least an email from your organisation, to thank them for their application and advise the candidate that they have not been shortlisted for an interview.

With those that have been shortlisted for interview you will be keen to get in touch with them promptly in order to arrange for them to attend interview. When candidates don't hear quickly and don't know your timetable from the advert, they may accept an offer elsewhere. Yuk!

Make sure that the letter that invites them to attend an interview is aimed at the Superstar audience.

Common Mistakes

Common mistakes we see are:

1. Letters that read as overformal and unfriendly. You are trying to attract someone to work with you not sentence them to prison!

2. Letters that are littered with mistakes. Commons irritations are names being spelt incorrectly, e.g, Mrs Edwards rather than Mrs Edmunds, names with hyphens being missed off, e.g. Siân spelled Sian. It's not difficult to achieve and sends out the right message that you do the important things well.

3. Poor grammar and letters that don't have dates on or one person's address and another first name. These are letters that look rushed and often are.

Don't assume it won't matter to the candidate. The Superstar will be informed about your organisation and your values by the communications you put out. Your job is to make sure that those communications are a credit to your organisation and not an embarrassment. Remember in addition to the Superstar others will see your letter. As individuals want to be shortlisted, the letter inviting them to attend an interview is very welcome when it arrived. As a consequence it is often shared with other members of the household. Your letter may be scrutinised by others who the Superstar candidate knows, loves and trusts, will they see the errors the Superstar missed?

With those candidates who are 'Maybes', and where you have not identified an interview date that you included in your advert, you will want to do one of two things;

1. Delay responding to them until you have secured the 'yes' candidates for interviews.
2. Respond to the list, thanking them for their application and advising you have had a large response and will be in touch. This is also known as the 'holding letter'.
3. Reject these candidates because you have enough Yes' to proceed to the next stage.

Once rejected there is no going back. If you do go back to the rejected candidates it would be to advise of another vacancy that you feel they may be suited for. Again don't assume that someone will be happy for you to keep their data on file to approach again in the future. Many people are not keen for their personal data to be retained these days. Always give someone the opportunity to ask you to remove their record from file and not use it for future vacancies.

Chapter 12

Designing & Planning the Interview

"Get the right people on the bus, the wrong people off the bus, and the right people in the right seats".

Jim Collins

Formats interviews can take include:

- Telephone Interviews
- Face to Face Interviews
- Skype Interviews

There are pro's and con's to these different formats.

Telephone interviews

These are quick to arrange and involve usually just the candidate and the interviewer. Candidates are often nervous of this format as they can't see who is interviewing them. It can lead to very 'stilted' responses as the candidate is lacking the ability to see your reaction to their answers. They cost little money to hold and can be very flexible for both the candidate and interviewer. For me telephone interviews work best when the candidate would spend time on the telephone every day. If that is not an essential skill for the post, then I would not use the telephone interview.

Face to Face interviews

These are the most common format for interviews to take. They are sometimes difficult to co-ordinate and do have a cost associated with them, but in the main they are effective use of your time and resources. Employers expect to conduct face to face interviews, and potential employees expect to attend them. If you choose to combine other forms of interview along with face to face you will probably achieve your objectives. One of the disadvantages of attending face to face interviews for candidates is that they are often scheduled in the normal working day, and unlike in schools, Early Years' practitioners are not expected to reveal that they are seeking alternative employment.

Skype interviews

Using technology such as Skype or Facetime to interview candidates is a new introduction to the recruiter's options. It has the benefit of being efficient as neither party has to travel to the interview. Unfortunately being dependent on technology can mean that it lets you down when you least need it to. The webcam will only capture one interviewer at a time, the candidate can feel that they are being overheard by others who they cannot see (this is another criticism of telephone interviews conducted on a loud speaker).

One benefit is that they can be recorded and then the interview replayed at a later date. A disadvantage is that the candidate is unlikely to be relaxed and therefore you can end up hiring the person who best coped with the technology rather than the best candidate for the job.

In conclusion whilst useful and in some ways better than a telephone interview, they can't replace the effectiveness of face to face interviews.

The elements to designing an interview

There are three main elements to designing an interview for you to consider:

- Who will interview, this determines the style of interview to be used?
- Where will the interview take place?
- When will the interview take place?

Who should interview?

This is one of the most exciting phases of the selection process for the Manager as they get to do the interviews. Over the years a lot has been written about the overall effectiveness of interviews as a selection process. Whilst they may not be as reliable as other forms of selection, we don't want to lose them, because they are just so useful. After all, who would not want to meet their future staff in an interview before making them an offer? To me it boils down to basic human need, we need to work with people so therefore meeting them in an interview environment allows us to get to know them and see whether we could imagine working with them in the future.

The style of interview is a very important consideration. At this point you may have several people indicating that they just must be on the interview for X position.

You should always consider requests such as this carefully. Some people who are keen to be involved in the selection decision are not doing this in the best interests of the Nursery. Again I have often seen this where the best candidate made another key member of the team look inferior, what a surprise, they did not support their appointment.

Those who will be inducting the new staff member are often best placed to interview. As I shall describe later, the induction is just an extension of the selection process and the candidate will still be forming impressions about their new employer.

Those who have a day to day knowledge of the workings of the Nursery make good interviewers. Anyone who is not involved in the day to day running can miss responses that to those who will work with the new colleague could be of concern.

The Style choices are:

- 1 to 1
- Duo
- Panel

To identify whether you have a Superstar for your Nursery in front of you is no mean feat, and you want to put your very best recruiters in the interview room.

I would recommend 'duo' interviews, i.e. two interviewers for most positions. The only exception we would see for an Early Years Teacher where a panel interview (three interviewers) would be appropriate due to the competencies required for the job.

Pick individuals who have received training in interviewing techniques and at least one interviewer should be competent in Safer Recruitment as well.

Where and when to interview?

We recommend interviewing your Superstar in your setting, ideally when you are open. A Superstar will want to use all their senses when forming an opinion of your setting. Senses of sight, sound, smell, touch are very important and you should ensure that your setting presents itself in the very best way before the candidate arrives.

There can be reasons why interviews take place after 6 p.m. in the evening, availability of the candidate may be one, and availability of interviewers can be another.

I recommend it pays to be flexible when booking an interview. A non-Superstar will tell you the will come at 11 a.m. as "Its Ok, I'll call in sick!", a Superstar will be bothered about their current commitment to their employer and want to be able to attend your interview with the least possible disruption to the employer they are currently performing for.

Make sure other people who are not interviewing, know that interviews are taking place. Ensure you will not be disturbed during the interview.

You may also want to think about:

- Ensuring the candidates sign in on arrival, perhaps not in the Visitors book due to concerns over the confidentiality of other candidates.
- Making a sign for the door "Interview in Progress"
- Is there a coat rack for the candidate to place their outdoor clothing?
- Having somewhere for candidates to sit if the room is not quite ready
- Having an interview room set up, tidy and free from distractions.
- Having water and glasses on the table.
- Making sure some will get the Nursery phone if it rings.

Involving the Children

Many settings choose to involve the children in interview process and it is considered good practice. Perhaps you will choose to observe the candidates interacting with your children as part of the interview process. There can be three benefits to involving the children:

1. The candidate can be observed interacting with the children. How they are in the interview room, may not compare to how they are when working with the children.
2. The children's response to the adult can leave to further questions in the interview.
3. The candidate gets to see what working in your Day Nursery may involve. They are better

informed as to what it would be like when they reach their own decision.

An alternative is asking candidates to prepare an activity which they would use with a group of children that if selected, they would be working with.

Maybe some of your older children can help candidates to have a tour of your setting with some adult assistance?

How long should the interview be?

Interviews will differ in length depending on how many people are involved and the seniority of the position. Very few quality interviews would be less than 30 minutes long. The timings of the interview should be planned so there is time for everything that the interviewers want to cover with the candidate, whilst they have them in front of them. Superstars will not appreciate being messed about and brought back for more than two interviews. When a time schedule has been identified this information should be shared with the candidate in the correspondence to attend the interview. If you are planning on an interview of one hour you would want to tell the candidate that they need to be available for at least one hour. If you need them for an entire morning (i.e. for an assessment centre) this should also be made very clear to the candidate from the communications they have received.

What to send candidates about the interview?

In the letter you send to the candidates inviting them to attend the interview you should include instructions as to what you expect them to prepare in advance, whether you require them to bring passports, proof of identity with them to the interview, their original certificates (which you will copy) and any portfolio of their previous work. Leave nothing to guess work. You want to be able to compare 'cheese with cheese'.

If your location is not obvious you may want to include directions and/or a map. Perhaps details of where to park as a visitor will be useful to your candidates and prevent any awkward moments on arrival.

Other areas to include in your letter inviting them to attend are:

- Time and venue (especially important where you have more than one location.)
- Directions or a map to the venue.
- Who will be present, their names and job titles.
- Any specific task that has been set to assist in the selection process and the time/method allocated for this.
- Invite them to inform you of any special requirements they may have in order to participate in the selection process equally, (e.g. access, large print/Braille, interpreters).

The invitation to attend interview may be posted as a letter to your candidate. We still think this is a brilliant idea as many employers look to communicate by email and a written letter shows the time and effort was taken to invite you to attend. This is a matter of personal choice and there are no rules. If you choose to confirm arrangements by email, then that's absolutely fine.

The interviewer's role prior to the interview

Prior to the interview itself, the interviewers must familiarise themselves with the candidates application forms and prepare interview the questions. It works well if those interviewing (or the panel) get together before hand and agree who will ask what questions and what role each will play in the interview. Every interview needs one person who will 'Chair' the process and set the scene for the candidate, explaining how the interview will progress and what will happen after the interview.

They should also be familiar with the assessment system to be used and how they will 'score' the candidates at interview.

Spares

Someone will always misplace their interview information. Always have spares of the application form to hand, and it is polite to only have the candidate's application in front of you, and not have within sight of the candidate other applications forms. Copies of the Job Description and Person Specification will also be useful to have as spares. Pens have a habit of failing when you least expect it, so extra pens will also be a good idea.

Chapter 13

Conducting the Interview

The day of the interview has arrived. You are nervous. You think to yourself why am I nervous? I already have a job here. Then you realise that as an interviewer the spot light from the candidate's perspective will be on you and you don't want to 'muck it up!'

Building Rapport

After welcoming them to your setting and asking them to sign in your only aim now is to build rapport to set the candidate at ease. It also has the effect of setting you at ease if you are nervous. This is the general "chit chat" that goes on before an interview properly gets off the ground. Questions about their journey to you, whether they are familiar with the area, are all neutral questions which are easy to ask; and therefore easy to answer.

Choosing where you sit

Sit where you are comfortable. There are no hard and fast rules. Interviewing in your office may mean that space is at a premium and that you can see a lot of distractions whilst you interview.

Interviewing in the garden on a Summer's day may be a good idea, probably not if children are around. Always have something to lean on and perhaps a clipboard if no table is available.

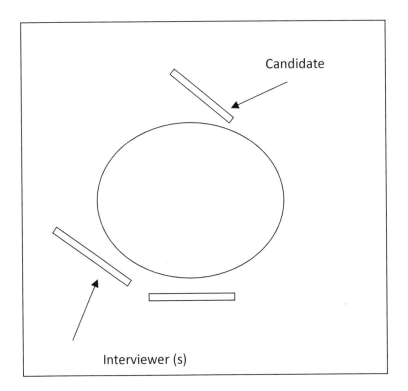

Figure 3

Keep paperwork about the other candidates away from the interviewee's line of sight, perhaps in a folder.

Have a plan for the interview and stick to it. It's more than professional to have an interview plan, don't worry if the candidates see this, it shows you are prepared.

Don't walk the candidate through their application form?

Over the years' I've seen many an interview experience wasted on a tour or the application form or CV. These interviews tend to go a bit like this:

- "I see you went to school locally, did you enjoy it?"
- "Was Miss Walton still the PE Teacher when you were there?"
- "You have 5 GCSE's, bet they seem ages ago now?"
- "What made you choose Geography as an option?"
- "Whilst at school you had a part time job in Superdrug?"
- "Great bargains in there compared to Boots"
- "You then did three years in the Baby Room at Little Smiles"
- "What did you like about that job?" " I see you left and went to work in Asda"
- "What made you choose Asda, we've got one of those just opened, not been there yet"

And it goes on....

Yes the interviewer is building rapport and seeking connections with the candidate, but the "good stuff" that could be gained by the interview is not being covered. The candidate knows their application form (if they completed it) and knows the chronological order in which they have had their live experiences.

It would have been more insightful to learn what the candidate learned from their experience of part time work at an early age; what they have gained from an experience in retail that they can use in a Day Nursery environment; why they left Little Smiles.

What questions to ask?

Questions should be prepared that assess and evaluate the applicant's suitability for the post against the criteria in the person specification.

In addition it would be a good idea to assess the following:

- The candidate's attitude towards children.
- His or her ability to support the organisation's commitment to safeguarding and promoting the welfare of children.
- Gaps in the candidate's employment history.

Wording effective questions

Hypothetical questions are those that begin with; "What would you do if…" and "Who would you speak to if…" With the hypothetical question the candidate is trying to anticipate the answer you seek and you will often get what I describe as a 'stock' answer.

Here's an example:

- What would you do if three year old child came to our Day Nursery who had no understanding of English and whose parents had only been in the

UK for a few weeks with only a few words of English?

Here you will get a 'stock' response, there would be no way of knowing whether that is what the candidate would do or whether the response is based on what they think you want to hear.

Words like inclusion are easy to use and difficult to demonstrate! What you want from the interview process is the ability to predict future performance. This is why the criteria based interview question is a great addition to your structure.

Criteria Based Questions

These are questions that seek to find evidence of future performance on the basis of past performance.

These questions will often start with one of two phrases;

- "Give me an example where"
- "Tell me about an occasion when"

Strictly speaking they are not questions but instructions. The candidate must recall a memory that tells the story of what you are looking to understand about them.

Here's an example:

"Tell me about an occasion when a child in your care developed a very high temperature?"

The response given by the Superstar candidate will be 'littered' with examples of good practice:

- "sought a second opinion"
- "followed our sick child policy"
- "stripped down to nappy"
- "applied cold compress"
- "gave cuddles and reassured child"
- "rang Mum and asked her to collect"

What you would feel from this response is how the candidate felt when they were dealing with this situation. You will get a sense of their relationship with their key children, and how they follow a setting's procedures in a caring and nurturing way.

What order to ask your questions?

Never go straight into the interview with a criteria based question. It's too much, too soon! Always build up to criteria based questions by asking the candidate questions that build rapport and some hypothetical questions, that they might have anticipate being asked.

I like to ask about their journey and whether they found us ok, at the same time establishing whether they know the area or are new to it.

After telling them about how the interview is structured I then ask them to tell me about themselves and get them talking about the person they know best, themselves!

Ask them to tell you something that they have learned about your Day Nursery; it will show whether they have read the Candidate Information Pack or visited your website.

Only after I can see they have relaxed into the interview process will I start to ask some hypothetical and then criteria based questions.

Always remember, they are interviewing you too!

It's worthwhile remembering that when you are interviewing your Superstar candidate, they are interviewing you. They will be forming impressions based on how prepared you are for the interview; how friendly you are, how structured the interview is, how well the interviewers are working together. Inadvertently you could give a negative impression and destroy your chances of hiring a Superstar for your Day Nursery.

Letting candidates know the outcome

It's a good idea to let candidates know the outcome of their interview within a few days of the interview. It would be unfair to leave a candidate (who may be attending several interviews) dangling waiting for a response. It would no doubt leave an unfavourable impression in your candidates mind, and they will share their negative experience with others that they know.

There have been instances where I have seen interviewers be what I describe as 'too hasty' with their response. The candidate finishes their interview at 4 p.m. and so unimpressed was the panel that the email rejecting their application after an interview was sent before 5 p.m. The argument being that they have made their decision and why delay. It doesn't look like much time was spent weighing up the positives and negatives of the candidate's application and would suggest that the candidate wasted their time.

Every candidate that has taken the time to attend an interview with you is owed a letter giving them the decision you have reached on their application. Its common courtesy and will always reflect positively on your brand. If you feel able to, offer to give feedback to the unsuccessful candidate. If you do not want to offer the feedback, at least be prepared to give it if the candidate seeks feedback. Again, it is the courteous thing to do.

Chapter 14

Other Selection Methods

Interviews aren't the only form of selection to be used. Other methods of selection can give you greater results. These can include:

- Assessment Centres.
- Trials.
- Psychometric and Personality Profiles.
- Skills Tests.

As with shortlisting, it is really important that you don't inadvertently discriminate when you are using these selection methods.

High risk methods include:

- Tests that require the candidate to have English as a first language.
- Tests that have to be handwritten if handwriting skills not an essential element of the post.
- Tests that include physical activities where the physical element is not an essential element of the post.
- Tests that require prior knowledge i.e. using software that the candidate may not have seen before.

Whatever you decide, its best practice to ensure that you have been honest and upfront with the candidate about the style of selection you are adopting. No one likes a nasty surprise and particularly a Superstar candidate who will not be impressed by an activity being sprung upon then. When this happens the only competency you are assessing is someone's ability to deal with a change in priority, and whilst a commendable skill for anyone to possess in a Day Nursery this may not be what you want to assess at all.

Using Assessment Centres

An assessment centre is where you bring a number of candidates back to work together in the selection process. These enable you to see team working and the ability of candidates to get along with each other in what is essentially an artificial situation.

Assessment Centres work best in circumstances where you needed to hire more than one Superstar. They could therefore be useful in these situations:

- Where you are opening a new setting.
- Where you are expanding and building a new room/department.
- Where you are replacing an entire team.
- Where you are taking over a setting after closure.
- Where you are taking over a new setting and only 'skeletal' staffing remains.

Assessment centres take a lot of planning. Candidates should be occupied for 80% of the time and the remaining 20% they should be able to relax and get to know their colleagues on the assessment centre. You are still observing them though.

Trials

Trials should be practical, planned with care and scored in the same way as the formal interview.

With trials:

- The candidate can be observed interacting with the children.
- Children's responses to the adult can be taken into account.
- The interviewee can get a feel for the workplace. Can they see themselves working there?
- The current staff will have the opportunity to meet and talk to potential staff. If they feel involved they are more likely to accept the appointment decision made.

It gives you the opportunity to show your Superstar candidate the working environment – working. It is not unusual for the children to be involved in the selection process. If you run a before and after school club you may even find that the older children want to prepare some questions to ask the short listed candidate.

Trials may last anything between an hour and a whole session (a.m. or p.m.) and are best if structured. They take time to organise and plan effectively and you should invite candidates to take part in a trial as part of the selection process.

The candidate may not be in a position to take a morning off work to attend your trial. In my opinion that should be respected. The Superstar candidate won't drop their current employer 'in it' just to attend an interview for the potential, future employer.

You would not normally pay for a candidate to attend a trial, though you may pay expenses, such as car parking, train fare or petrol. This is entirely at your discretion. I am tempted to support the expenses where it is a effectively their third interview with you.

Trials should be designed to assess certain competencies that you haven't been able to assess through the interview process. These will often include:

- Working with Others
- Working with the Children
- Planning and Organising

You will want to see whether the candidates share your values and beliefs. For example a candidate that is cutting out a child's work, or telling the child where to stick or put their mark, isn't supporting the child's learning they are stifling it. Whilst this isn't misconduct it's not want you want to see in a competent performer.

You may want to design in some feedback time into the trial session. Then you can ask the candidate to give you feedback on how they found the trial and whether they have any questions to ask you.

Be careful of the involvement of other staff in the selection process. As mentioned in Chapter 12 colleagues may not want you to hire a candidate who may show up their faults. We should always be aiming to surround ourselves with people who are better than us, but some colleagues seem to forget this principle when it suits them to do so.

Psychometric/Personality Profiles

These should always be administered by qualified and competent individuals and profiles should be used in conjunction with their copyright.

Profiles can be very insightful. Common ones include:

- Myers Briggs Indicator
- Belbin Team Types
- DISC
- Insights Colours Profile

If you determine to use a profile as part of the selection process you may need to broaden its use across other members of your team. This will allow you to compare the profiles and see whether you are completing your balanced team.

I would reserve the use of profiles for management roles and have found them very useful in the past. Expect to pay between £70 and £200 per profile you purchase.

Skills Tests

Skills tests or in tray exercises are very useful to determine whether someone understands their area of expertise. Organising three things into a priority order and being able to explain why, writing up an incident form, recording a parent complaint in a concise manner; all of these skills and many more can be assessed using a skills test. It is important that candidates understand in advance of the interview whether they will be asked to undertake a skills test. It would not be considered fair to launch into one without the candidate being prior warned. Some candidates may not reveal a disability to you until posed with a skills test that they know they can't complete on an 'equal playing ground'. For example a candidate may be dyslexic and require a reader. You wouldn't want to discover this in a 'live' situation.

A modern alternative to the in-tray is the inbox exercise, where the employer sets up a laptop with a inbox with emails in there that they would like the candidate to respond to. Emails are then forwarded with their responses. These kinds of exercises can demonstrate thought process and decision making, use of external resources, written English, prioritisation skills and time management.

Chapter 15

Making a Verbal Offer

I often think of this as the best part of the job. Hearing the delight in someone's voice down the end of the phone when you advise them that they are the successful candidate is a lovely feeling.

Your Superstar candidate will expect you to make the call in a professional manner, indicating the seriousness of the process to commence employment in your Day Nursery. They will still expect you to be friendly but will completely understand that you need to make the offer conditional.

Hopefully during the interview process you will have received the following from the candidate:

- Evidence of right to work in the UK.
- Evidence of original certificates.
- Enhanced DBS, hopefully they will be a member of the Update Service already and will have given you their Update Service Number and invited you to check the status of the enhanced disclosure on line.

Not every candidate will have the right to work in the UK. You are not meant to become an expert in all things border and immigration, but you should know to ask for evidence of someone's right to work in the UK.

You can hire someone before you receive their DBS enhanced disclosure certificate, but if you do, you need to bear in mind that you will not be able to allow them to work unaccompanied with children until the DBS is received, and you may experience period of delay at certain times of the year. As DBS becomes the norm, we imagine this problem will be avoided as individuals will have joined the Update Service and will be quite happy to allow you to establish the status of the DBS by you going online.

Original certificates are very important. Plenty of employers have hired someone subject to sight of original certificates and them been told the certificate is lost. We appreciate that awarding bodies charge for new certificates to be issued, but as an employer you need to be firm and insist that the certificate is obtained. There are a number of fake childcare certificates in circulation. You should do everything in your capacity to ensure you are not deceived.

Never accept written references from the candidate. Anyone who brings their references with them, unless the employer has gone out of business should be advised that you will still need to write to two referees using your reference request forms. Unfortunately, too many of these *To Whom It May Concern* references are fake.

When making a verbal offer I recommend that you take yourself to a quiet room where you will not be disturbed to make the call. You may mishear what the candidate has to say if your environment is noisy. If you find such calls difficult, try standing up to make the call. When we stand up we sound more assertive on the telephone and we don't have the difficulty in breathing that we may experience when slouched at a desk!

I use a checklist in Figure 4 to make sure that nothing is missed during the call.

Be Cool

Don't rush this conversation.

Always 'check in' with the candidate before announcing your news. Invite them to give you feedback about how they felt after their interview with you. I am afraid it is not uncommon for candidates to reject employment. Sometimes their employer has made them a better offer, sometimes they thought about the role and have decided it's not for them.

Remember to be polite if the candidate rejects the position. They are rejecting the post not you; they may have many reasons for reaching this decision. It may this is not the right time. It may be not a never situation, just not now. Don't lose good candidates by reacting negatively. If you do argue or react rudely they will tell others, and these may be people you would want to attract to your Day Nursery.

Verbal Offer Checklist

Name:

Position:

Interview Date:

Telephone No.:

1. Greet the candidate.
2. Explain that you have news following the interview.
3. Ask how they felt after the interview/trial etc? Respond to any questions. Bear in mind they may reject you at this point.
4. If applicable, say you have some "good news" and you have been asked to call them today to make a verbal conditional offer.
5. Explain the conditions of that verbal offer*

   a. Enhanced DBS certificate
   b. 2 references
   c. Evidence of original certificates.
   d. Evidence of right to work in UK.
   e. Completion of the 3/6 month probationary period.

6. Outline the terms and conditions, of the post.
7. Ask whether they would like to accept verbal offer.
8. If applicable, ask when they would be available to start.
9. Confirm offer will be sent in writing and whether an email or letter.
10. Explain if they will need to respond in writing to written offer.
11. Agree when you will be in touch again.
12. Close the call.

Verbal Offer made by:...

Date: ....

*Some of these won't be applicable as you will have seen evidence already. Delete as appropriate.

Figure 4

When finishing the call. Thank the candidate for their time and confirm what happens next. If you wish them to take action, be clear as to what that action is. Never assume that candidates know what is expected of them.

If you would like them to respond to the written offer, advise them of such. Perhaps they can email an acceptance rather than putting it in writing.

Many candidates won't be able to confirm a start date with you until they have received your written offer. Equally they will be reluctant to resign from their current employment until they have read your offer and have it 'in their hands'. This isn't the Superstar candidate being funny with you, this is the Superstar protecting their interests, in the same way you expect them to operate in your best interests going forward.

A Superstar candidate may be hard for another employer to lose. It is not uncommon for individuals to withdraw following an offer after they have advised their current employers that they are leaving. Employers may be tempted to make a counter offer to avoid the cost of recruitment. Again it is reasonable to feel aggrieved by a candidate who rejects you in order to accept an improved offer where they are. Hopefully it won't happen very often to you, it does happen, and I am afraid there is very little an employer can do about it.

If you are going to email them an offer, check that this is acceptable to them, especially if it is possible that the email address is a shared account.

Lizandcolin@gmail.com.

This is a clue that Liz and Colin perhaps share their email account. What would happen if you emailed an offer, and Liz hadn't told Colin she was attending interviews? Very embarrassing and not a great start to the employment relationship!

Chapter 16

Making a Written Offer

Like the verbal offer conditional written offers of employment should only be written by authorised personnel. If the verbal offer went well; you will now want to seize the initiative and write to the candidate and make a written offer. The offer must be conditional on the following being achieved to the satisfaction of the employer:

- Two satisfactory references, if not already obtained.
- Proof of right to work in the UK, if not already obtained.
- An Enhanced Disclosure Certificate from the Disclosure and Barring Service that is to the satisfaction of the employer. This could be reviewing their certificate online if they are a member of the Update Service.
- Verification of original certificates that support employment.
- Medical Examination (if applicable, for some posts this may be part of the selection process, for a candidate to pass a medical with an independent medical examiner.)
- Completion of the employer's probationary period.

Letters of offer can be emailed to a candidate, so long as you have the facility to either print a letter on your letter head, which you can then sign and scan to send to the candidate; or that you can save a letter as a pdf file. The importance of the pdf file is that it cannot be amended by the candidate.

Ideally you can send a letter of offer by First Class post to your candidate in a smart envelope and continue to create and maintain the right first impression with the candidate.

With most candidates, and particularly our Superstar candidate they will not resign from their current employment until they have sight of your written offer. Who can blame them? What if the verbal offer was delivered incorrectly? Sadly some candidates will use a written offer to negotiate a better deal with their current employer. There is nothing you can do about this, so don't waste mental bandwidth worrying about it.

The letter of offer should seek their confirmation that they are accepting the offer. There are several options in how you can go about gaining their acceptance.

1. Ask them to sign and return one copy of the letter of offer (include two copies in the envelope)
2. Ask them to write to you to confirm their acceptance. An email may be a quicker response.
3. Ask them to telephone you to indicate their decision and discuss a start date. This isn't ideal, we would hope that if you had been able to make a verbal offer that start dates could be provisionally agreed, if this was not the case, this would be

satisfactory, but we would ideally have written confirmation before the first day of employment.

If you don't hear back from the candidate, do get in touch by one of their other contact details. Letters do go astray. You wouldn't want to assume a candidate is not interested until you hear from the candidate themselves. Situations do sometimes change, so do remember not to show your frustration if the candidate does withdraw at this late stage, remember the impression you want to be leave.

Written Statement of Terms and Conditions

Along with the written offer, the candidate should be supplied with a Written Statement of Terms and Conditions. I know some employers wait to issue this document until after the probationary period. This is a potentially risky move, as under the Employment Rights Act 1996, the employee has the right to receive these written statements within 8 weeks of their employment starting. Few probationary periods are just 8 weeks long.

The Written Statement of Terms and Conditions gives the employee the information they need, accompanied by their written offer, in order to know whether they wish to accept the offer of employment. Without reading the Written Statement they may not be aware of any conditions, requirements or terms that are expressed in the Written Statement and may affect the employee's wish to accept the offer.

The Written Statement of terms and conditions is the contract of employment, which forms the basis of the employer, employee relationship.

The following details must be included in the Written Statement of Terms and Conditions:

- The Employer's name
- The Employee's name
- The Job Title or a Brief Job Description
- The date employment began, the place of work, and the address where employment will take place.
- The amount of pay and interval between payments.
- Hours of work
- Holiday pay entitlement.
- Sick Pay arrangements.
- Pension arrangements.
- Notice periods.
- Where not permanent, the period employment is expected to continue.
- Disciplinary rules
- Grievance arrangements.
- Any collective agreements that may be in place.

In addition we recommend you seek advice from a HR professional experienced in preparing Written Statements for employers in the Early Years' sector. You would want to include sections or clauses that cover;

- Disclosure and Barring Service Disclosures
- Third Party Pressure to Dismiss
- Declarations that refer to working with children.

Chapter 17

Taking References

References are the third element of the selection triangle. Without one element of the selection triangle and it is said that your selection is incomplete.

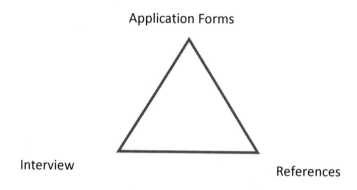

Figure 5

The Superstar candidate may well have anticipated your need for references and will have approached previous employers to find out how they can be utilised as a referee. A poor candidate will not have any idea who is the best person to respond to your reference request and will often not know what address that you should use for your request either.

There is no requirement for references to be contacted by the candidate prior to being used, but it is definitely considered polite.

There are two types of reference that we use in selection processes:

- Professional/Work references
- Character References.

If the candidate has not worked before but has studied at school or college, the referee will often be a college tutor/ Head of Department, and they will be giving a character reference. It would not be acceptable for a reference to be supplied by a fellow student on the same course.

If I had to choose I would much rather be influenced by a reference provided in a work context than a character reference.

I've never read a character reference that wasn't positive. In fact most are completely glowing!

Why seek references?

The purpose of seeking references is to enable you to obtain factual information to support your appointment decisions.

You are looking for information that is inconsistent with information you have gathered at earlier stages of the selection process.

For example:

Emma has completed an application form and advised you that she was a Room Leader for her current employer between March 2013 and May 2014, a period of 14 months. You see that experience as vital as you are keen to hire qualified individuals who are capable of running a room or department.

The reference comes back and states that she was Room Leader for a period of three months between March 2013 and May 2013.

When asked about it she says it was an admin error. You may accept this fact but you may also find that her responses to her achievements in the period she was Room leader to be less trustworthy and you may now be thinking that she has tried to deceive you.

Similarly I have seen candidates whose' references have identified the following discrepancies:

- Dismissed rather than redundant
- Assistant Manager rather than Manager.
- Part qualified rather than qualified.

Most commonly the reason for leaving and the dates of employment/time in post will vary.

This can be down to administration errors but is often someone trying to give you false information. You will find that many references limit themselves to confirming the following:

- Name
- Job Title
- Dates of Employment
- Reason for Leaving

This will sometimes be referred to as a 'tombstone' reference. They are of use, regardless of what you may feel for the reasons I described above. Gaining factual information that enables you to validate the information you have already obtained and will always be useful.

Gaining Consent to approach referees

It is important that candidates give you consent to approach their references, particularly if you intend to approach these before an offer of employment is made.

This is the approach commended in Safer Recruitment courses and is common practice in Schools. I have seen many a candidate embarrassed that their Nursery Manager has received a reference request when they hadn't even told their Nursery Manager they were looking for work.

I recommend including a box in the application form showing that the referee can be approached.

References: Please give **TWO** referees (one of whom should be your current or last employer) If you do **NOT** wish us to contact either referee before an offer is made, please place a cross in the appropriate box.			
Name	Address	Telephone Number	Email Address
☐			
☐			

Figure 6

If a reference comes back that is not to your satisfaction you should discuss it with the candidate. It may be there is an explanation for the reference. I have known Managers to write less than positive references because they don't want to lose their Superstar performer. I am afraid it is a sad reflection on the Manager. Always get the reference signed and get the referee's name.

What to ask on your reference request forms?

It is important to develop a form for both professional and character references. As well as being professional you are more likely to get a reference back if you have made it easy for the referee to give the reference.

A work reference will need different questions than a character reference, if you use the same form, the character reference may have to mark the reference, not applicable in several sections.

You may ask the Superstar's referee about the following aspects of their performance and conduct at work:

- Length of Service
- Time in post
- Role performed in the previous employer
- Whether they were a supervisor?
- Reason for leaving
- Previous Salary
- Number of days absent in the previous twelve months*
- Whether they are suitable to work with children?

*This question **may not** be asked **prior** to an offer being made since the introduction of the Equality Act 2010.

You may choose to include the Job Description and Person Specification for the vacancy to assist the referee to answer these questions. In addition to a reference request form, many employers attach a separate letter to accompany the reference.

One of the reasons why I increasingly see Day Nurseries request their references by email is for this reason. Individuals receiving a request may be more likely to respond promptly to an email rather than a letter which requires more action.

Email addresses for referees are fine, but I would like to see alison.lee@smileynurseries.co.uk rather than alison.lee@btinternet.com for obvious reasons.

As part of safeguarding you should ask the referee whether they have any reason to doubt the candidate's suitability to work with children. If they do they should be invited to give specific details of why they believe the person may be unsuitable.

You should remind the referee that:

- They have a responsibility to ensure the reference is accurate and does not contain any material misstatement or omission.
- Relevant factual content of the reference may be discussed with the applicant.

Referees can mark their reference as confidential.

There an urban myth that referees cannot give bad references. They can if it means that the person has been bad!

The general rule of thumb with references is that the referee can't reveal anything to the new employer that is not already known to the person the reference is about.

Here's an example of this in action:

Donna was causing her employer some concerns. The employer wrote in the reference that she would have been dismissed if she had not resigned. This was not known to Donna and therefore was an unfair reference.

If the job offer had been withdrawn on the back of this reference, Donna may very well have had a claim against her previous employer over the reference that was given.

Employers should make sure:

- That only authorised Manager's give references. Develop a Reference Policy if required.
- That they always have the consent of the employee/ex-employee to give a reference (this can be covered at exit interview)
- That they take care to give the new employer an accurate reference.
- That they do not say anything in a reference that is not known to the individual.
- Keep a record of the reference they return.

What if you experience difficulty obtaining a reference?

I always will ask the candidate to assist you with this. If you have offered a position subject to two written references and you are experiencing difficulties, I would ask the candidate to intervene. This is especially true of their character reference. If they are not responding, should they have asked them to be their referee and could someone else be used. If a candidate is reliant on a character reference they may have a selection of people who could perform this function for them:

- Scout Leaders.
- Head Teachers/ Department Heads/ College Lecturers.
- Police Officers.
- Paramedics/Doctors/Dentists.
- MPs/Magistrates/Solicitors.

With younger candidates it is common to find that the character reference is a friend of the family rather than a personal friend of the candidate. They will often have known the candidate over a number of years and have seen them growing up. Character references will often take the performance of this responsibility very seriously and reply promptly. If there is a delay; it is often down to miscommunication, holiday or ill health.

Will telephone references be satisfactory?

A telephone reference is quite a difficult thing to achieve. Employers are quite rightly concerned to give out verbal references over the telephone. They do not know who they are speaking to. Saying that, as an employer if you are finding it difficult to get a response from a referee a telephone call into that reference will often pay you dividends.

You can find the following when you ring:

- That there are no records at hand for the reference to be completed.
- That there is no-one working there that remembers your candidate.
- That it is Company policy not to give references.
- That sadly references cannot be completed locally and that it has been referred to Head Office.
- That the HR Department is on holiday/shut.
- That they have no record of your request/can't find the letter you sent.

Always ask who you are speaking to and make a note of their name.

If you can obtain a verbal reference you may be very lucky. You should make a careful note of wat you are told as this may be the only professional reference you obtain for this candidate. Ofsted would prefer to see written references, but if you can show what you have done to provide two references this may satisfy your inspector.

Always thank the referee for their time.

If you are told that 'off the record' you should be nervous of employing X you need to consider whether you will be able to rely upon this reference.

The Company's position with the candidate was that the job offer was subject to two written references that were to the satisfaction of the Company. If this can't be achieved you should ask the candidate to assist you.

If the candidate can't 'chase their references' for you and you make a call into the ex-employer and they refuse to provide a reference, you are within your rights to withdraw the conditional offer. However ask yourself is this another organisation's policies impacting your ability to resource your Day Nursery?

As I mentioned earlier in this Chapter, I have known Manager's give a bad reference to try and keep an employee they didn't want to lose. Could this be happening in your situation?

What if allegations are made?

If the reference does suggest that allegations have been made regarding the individuals suitability to work with children, you should immediately raise this with the referee. They may be reluctant to discuss this with you but will normally be able to direct you to further information. If someone has been dismissed, perhaps you can ask to see the letter of dismissal from the candidate so you can understand for yourself why their employment came to an end.

If you determine that references are not acceptable the employer can withdraw the offer of employment. If employment has started this may be (if employment has been longer than one month) with statutory notice of one week. If in any doubt please discuss with a HR professional who can advise you further.

Chapter 18

The Probationary Period

The first three to six months of a new employee's employment will often be referred to as a formal probationary period.

The probationary period is not a phrase from employment law. It is a Human Resources term to cover that period of employment where the employment is not confirmed and is subject to a probationary period.

Reasons for having a probationary period include:

- Wanting a formal period where the employee and employer are getting to know each other.
- Wanting to delay certain benefits until the probationary period has been completed, due to the cost of benefits being awarded only for the candidate to leave during the initial period of employment.

Initial training

During the probationary period the new employee may well receive initial training, without which they cannot progress fully into their role. From a safeguarding perspective this may include child protection training, training in your whistleblowing procedure, training in terms of how you safeguard children.

Remaining vigilant

Despite your robust recruitment procedure you should remain vigilant in the probationary period. You may need to 'iron out some wrinkles' here even with the Superstar candidate.

Perhaps the candidate lacked sufficient experience working with the age of children you are asking them to work with now. It is not uncommon for an individual who is experienced in a pre-school room to find working with two year olds a challenge, and for them to misunderstand what is age appropriate. You may need to remind them of their training during the probationary period, if you don't want to store problems up for a later date.

Use the probationary period to provide training and information into your policies and procedures. Support individuals through Supervision. It may be your policy to hold Supervision meetings at set intervals. I would suggest these intervals may need to be closer in the following situations:

- During probationary periods.
- After a period of leave from employment (for example the group known as women returners).
- After a period when they have away from the workplace through sickness absence.
- Following a sabbatical.
- Following an internal promotion.

An individual may not perform during the probationary period, and the employer may need to consider whether the probationary period should be extended or whether the individual's contract should be terminated.

To do this fairly, the probationary period should be referred to in the Written Statement of Terms and Conditions.

A clause similar to this may be useful:

Probationary Period

Your employment is subject to an initial three month probationary period. If your employment is not to our satisfaction during the probationary period the Company reserves the right to extend the probationary period or terminate employment during the probationary period.

Figure 7

The employer may monitor performance and if the performance does not meet expectation may determine to extend the probationary period. A three month probationary period may be extended by a further three months, bringing the total probationary period to six months. It would be unusual to extend more than once. We advise our clients who ask about a further extension whether this would be the fair thing to do, and more often than not, as performance is not meeting their expectations, despite the first extension, the decision is taken to terminate the employment during the probationary period.

Chapter 19

The Induction

All too often I hear of inductions that consist of nothing more than an hour on the first day of employment. The induction phase of the employment cycle is a critical stage and should be led by the same individuals who led on the interview and selection stage. The recognition that the same people are involved gives the Superstar candidate confidence in the employer.

Inductions are to be designed to ensure the swift and effective introduction of the individual into the organisation and their new role.

During the first three months of employment, the individual is at most risk of leaving in what is often described as 'induction crisis'.

This is the period when they are making up their mind about their new employer, and vice versa, the new employer is making up their minds about the new employee. If an employee leaves during induction crisis they may be able to 'lose' the period of employment from their CV. They may go back to the interview process with other employers and forget about their 'spell' of employment with you. To avoid induction crisis, the employer must design an effective induction and to be able to demonstrate to the Superstar hire that all that was said during the selection process is true.

An effective induction will include:

- Tour of the premises, introductions to colleagues (even those they may rarely work with)
- An organisational overview, this is our history, this is where we are now, and this is where we are going.
- Time for the new employee to reflect and absorb the information they are being presented with.
- Time to meet new colleagues and get to know them, ideally some team building and opportunities for new teams to integrate.
- A section on whistleblowing and who to speak to if they have any concerns, no matter how small.
- Overview of facilities, remember individuals are motivated when they feel secure, safe and that their basic needs will be met. Show the new employees where they can make a drink, where the mugs live, where they can store their coat and bag, where the toilets are. Never assume these things don't matter or that someone else will show the new employee.
- A mentor/buddy to support the new employee. This is particularly impact where there is just one new starter starting in the Day Nursery. Ideally synchronise new starts so they share a first day, if this can't happen appoint a mentor/buddy to look after the new employee and be their contact.

- Structured training and an opportunity to learn what is expected of them through the policies and procedures of the Day Nursery.

- Training that recognises that we all learn differently. Some learners are visual and are quite happy reading policies and procedures, others are auditory and will enjoy listening to someone speak about your policies and procedures, further individuals (often more than 33%) will be practical learners and need to experience to learn. They will need you to run quizzes, practical exercises in groups, getting their hands on your policies and procedures and using them in practice.

- A HR overview, with someone explaining the issue of the Employee Handbook, who they will be paid, collecting employee details form information, explaining how payslips will be issued and how to book a holiday and report absence.

- A safety overview, with someone pointing out fire exits, fire assembly point and the general safety rules of the Day Nursery. A new starter should also experience a fire evacuation procedure during their induction. Simple things like we do not bleach into the toilet on top of the cleaning product, we store chemicals in this area, this is the COSHH kit to clean up spills. This is where PPE lives that you may need to use...

- An opportunity to give feedback as to how they have found the induction, so you know what is working and what needs more work.

Use an induction checklist and ask the individual to sign off their induction, whether this is element by element or as a whole. Manual Handling training will feature where and when to use step stool and that standing on furniture is never acceptable. I have known a signature on an induction checklist to save an employer from an insurance claim because the employer could demonstrate that the new employee had received health and safety instruction during the induction.

Made in the USA
Columbia, SC
03 August 2017